**HP**
HARDPRESS.NET
HOME OF HARD-TO-FIND BOOKS

# A Tour to the Isle of Wight
by Charles Tomkins

Address:
HardPress
8345 NW 66TH ST #2561
MIAMI FL 33166-2626
USA
Email: info@hardpress.net

Dup. to C.O.B
Be Kept (ish)
Turk.

# *A TOUR*

## TO THE

# ISLE OF WIGHT,

### ILLUSTRATED WITH

## EIGHTY VIEWS,

### DRAWN AND ENGRAVED IN AQUA TINTA.

### BY

## *CHARLES TOMKINS.*

### IN TWO VOLUMES.

### VOL. I.

### London:

PRINTED FOR G. KEARSLEY, FLEET-STREET.

1796.

TO

Sir JOHN BARRINGTON, Bart.

OF BARRINGTON HALL,

IN THE COUNTY OF ESSEX,

AND OF SWAINSTON, IN THE ISLE OF WIGHT,

MEMBER OF PARLIAMENT,

FOR THE BOROUGH OF NEWTOWN,

THIS TOUR

TO THE

*ISLE OF WIGHT,*

ILLUSTRATED WITH VIEWS,

IS DEDICATED,

WITH RESPECT, AND GRATITUDE,

FOR THE ENCOURAGEMENT AND ASSISTANCE

HE KINDLY AFFORDED THE AUTHOR,

IN THE PROGRESS OF THIS WORK,

BY HIS OBLIGED,

AND OBEDIENT SERVANT,

*CHARLES TOMKINS.*

# PREFACE.

IT was not the original intention of the Author to have given any more than a fhort account of each of the views, which he prefented to the public ; but finding, that though there were feveral hiftories of the Ifland, fóme of them were become fcarce, and none contained any direction, by which the traveller could guide his fteps, in fearch of the many beautiful fituations abounding in the Ifland, he was induced to change his purpofe, and after giving the beft hiftorical account, which he could feleæt, for the narrow limits of his work, and adding fome particulars not mentioned by former writers, he has fubjoined a complete

defcription of the country, by which the
reader may have an opportunity of going
through the Ifland, without miffing any
object that is worthy of his attention.

He begs the Subfcribers will have the
goodnefs to attribute the little delays
which have taken place in the publication of fome of the numbers, to the
anxiety which he has felt, to render his
work as complete as poffible, and to the
labour, which they will readily conceive,
muft reft upon a fingle individual, in fo
arduous a tafk, as the drawing and engraving eighty plates.

# DIRECTIONS

## FOR PLACING THE PRINTS.

## VOL. I.

# A
# TOUR
## TO THE
# ISLE OF WIGHT.

HAVING long been actuated by a defire to view the picturefque beauties of the *Ifle of Wight*, fo juftly called, by all who have vifited it, the *Garden of England*, I determined to embrace fo favourable a feafon as the fummer of 1793, to examine that beautiful and romantic ifland. I therefore left London early in June, and took the road for Southampton, through Kenfington and Hammerfmith, places too well known by their contiguity to the metropolis, to require any minute defcription. I next came to Brentford, the county-town of Middlefex, remarkable only for the length, dirtinefs, and ruggednefs of its ftreets. It has indeed been rendered memorable by the victory which Edmund Ironside obtained over the Danes, who raifed the fiege of London, in order to meet his army at this place, A.D. 943; hither alfo King Charles I. advanced after the battle of Edgehill, in 1642.

Three miles farther weftward is Houn-flow, a market town, principally inhabited by inn-holders, as it is the firft ftage on the great weftern road. Here I unfuccefsfully endeavoured to difcover the fcite of a convent of Friars of the order of the Holy Trinity, for the redemption of captives, which is faid to have exifted at this place before the third of Edward I.

This order carries the name of its in-ftitutor or founder, who was John of Matha, born at Provence, in France, in the year 1154. He followed his ftudies at Aix, and at Paris, where he took his degrees, and being afterwards made a prieft, he retired to a place near Maux, called

Cufroid, where, with an hermit, whofe name was Felix, he led a folitary life.

Both having been admonifhed in a dream, as the Papifts affirm, to go to Pope Innocent the IIId. they accordingly vifited Rome, where, the Pope having had the fame vifion, waited for them. On the preceding day, whilft he was faying mafs, it is faid, a hideous phantom appeared to him, arrayed in white, with a crofs half red and half blue on his breaft, and grafping, with his hands, two flaves bound in chains. This vifion made him refolve to eftablifh an order, whofe care fhould be, to go and redeem the Chriftian captives detained in flavery by the infidels. Having then conferred with the two hermits, he made them take an habit like to that which the phantom appeared in while he was at the altar, and gathering great alms, he fent them to redeem feveral captives, an undertaking which fucceeded very well, and induced many others to follow their example;

monafteries were alfo founded for them, where they profeffed the rule of St. Auftin. Their order was confirmed in the year 1207, under the name of the Holy Trinity, for the redemption of captives.

In England, this order was received in the year 1357, and was called the order of Ingham.

Hence I proceeded, acrofs Hounflow-Heath, to Bedfont. The church ftands on the right hand, at the entrance of the village; and the yew-trees which are before it, being cut in the fhape of two large birds, have a fingularly fantaftical appearance, and re-lieve the eye of the traveller, after having paffed three miles over a barren and un-cultivated heath.

Next to this is Staines, a market town, fixteen miles diftant from London, and fituated at the weftern extremity of Middle-fex, which is here divided from Surry by the river Thames. This place is greatly reforted to by perfons who prefer angling as an amufement; the river abounding with fifh, and its banks fupplying many convenient ftations for fportfmen of that defcription. In the meadows, which fkirt the river on each fide, are delightful walks; and in one of them, on the Middlefex fide, is an ancient ftone, placed by the corporation of London, to mark the boundary of their jurifdiction on the Thames. This place will be greatly improved in its appearance, by the ftone-bridge which is now erecting.

Croffing the Thames into Surry, the meadow on the right hand is Runnymede, the well-known fpot where King John figned *Magna Charta*, the foundation of our liberties, and of that happy Conftitution, which has ever been the wonder and admiration of Europe, the glory and pride of Englifhmen. This meadow is now the race-ground of Egham.

At a fhort diftance on the road, is the village of Egham, which was one of the firft poffeffions of Chertfey-Abbey. Abbot Rutheric, famous for his public works, built the chancel of the church in the time of Edward III.; the church itfelf however is much more ancient. Here lived the poet Sir John Denham, well known by his elegant defcription of Cowper's-hill, which is in this neighbourhood.

Leaving Windfor-foreft on the right, I next afcended Egham-hill, and entered the dreary heath of Bagfhot. Here the continued fandy road, and fucceffion of hills covered with dark furze, render travelling tirefome, and prove very ungratifying to the eye. This, at length, is fomewhat relieved by the artificial cafcade in Windfor Great Park, which, though the head of a confiderable piece of water, for want of proper management, is feparated into a confufed number of fmall ftreams, and hence is deftitute of that grandeur, of which fo magnificent an object might be rendered capable. Purfuing my journey over the heath, I paffed Sunninghill-wells, and arrived at Bagfhot, a fmall village, adjoining to which is Bagfhot-park, once the refidence of the late Prince of Wales. This, though fmall, is remarkably well wooded, and prefents a rich and lively fcenery, fcarcely any trees being vifible within feveral miles of it.

Leaving Bagfhot, and afcending a long hill, a lone houfe prefents itfelf, which is faid to have obtained the name and fign of the *Golden Farmer*, by the following extraordinary circumftance. A farmer, for feveral years, met his landlord at Bagfhot, for the purpofe of paying his rent, and taking advantage of the old man's convivial difpofition, always contrived to detain him till a late hour. When they feparated, the farmer difguifed himfelf, and knowing his landlord muft afcend the hill in his way home, he lay in wait for him at this place, and for feveral years robbed him of the bag of gold he had paid him but a few hours before. Playing this game, however, a little too often, he was at length detected in the fact, and confeffed, that he had, for a feries of years, paid his landlord the identical gold with which he had difcharged his firft year's rent.

Four miles farther, I croffed the ftream which parts Surry from Hampfhire at Blackwater, on leaving which, I kept a fine level road over the heath for near five miles, in a direct line to Hartford-bridge, and thence through the villages of Hartley-row, Hook-Newnham, and Skewers. Here the country becomes well wooded and cultivated. A few miles weftward, on the right, is the village of Bafing, at which was fought a bloody battle between the Saxons, under Ethelred and his brother Alfred, and the Danes, who obtained the victory A.D. 871. At Bafing, John Marquis of Winchefter, had a magnificent refidence, larger

than that of any other subject in the kingdom. It afterwards became a garrison for
King Charles I. and endured a siege of two
years, under its gallant and loyal lord; but
being at length entered by the Parliament
forces in 1645, it was plundered and burnt
to the ground by order of Oliver Cromwell.
All that can now be discovered of this magnificent habitation, are the garden walls,
and the scite, which is circular, like a keep,
with an area in the middle.

Before I entered Basingstoke, I crossed the
new canal, which is to join the river Wey,
near Chertsey, in Surry. Great difficulties
have arisen in the prosecution of this impor-
tant and laudable work, from the loose
sandiness of the soil, which the canal is un-
avoidably obliged to pass through: when
completed, however, it will be of essential
service, not only to the town of Basingstoke,
but to all the villages near which it passes.

c

Bafingftoke is forty-feven miles from London. It is governed by a corporation, and has a good market for corn and malt, and likewife poffeffes a fmall fhare of the woollen trade. It has a handfome church, built by Fox, Bifhop of Winchefter, in the reign of Henry VIII. as appears by an ancient infcription on the fpandrils of the north door of the chancel. The veftry and library adjoining, are parts of the old church; the library having been originally the chapel of St. Stephen. In this church were buried the mother and feveral of the kindred of Walter de Merton, Bifhop of Rochefter, and High Chancellor of England, the munificent founder of Merton-college, Oxford, in the reign of Edward I. A chauntry was founded for them in St. Stephen's chapel. Walter de Merton had large property and connections here. Sir George Wheeler, the great Afiatic traveller, was vicar of this church. The advowfon, being part of the poffeffions of Selbourne priory, was granted to Magdalen college, Oxford, by the founder, Bifhop William of Wainflete.

According to Tanner, Henry III. at the defire of Walter de Merton, founded an hofpital for aged priefts, at Bafingftoke. The walls were of flint, and part of the chapel-roof lately remained. It was panelled with the arms of Merton, in the interfections; but every mark of antiquity about this hofpital, was at length deftroyed by the erection of a new brick-building on the fpot, about the year 1778.

Here was born John de Bafingftoke, archdeacon of Leicefter, much celebrated for his knowledge of the Greek language, and an intimate friend of Matthew Paris; alfo Bifhop Grofthead, who firft introduced the Greek numerals into England. John de Bafingftoke died in 1252.

North of Bafingftoke, on the right of the road, is a foundation of Sir William Sands,

knight, chamberlain, and privy counſellor
to Henry VIII. who created him Lord Sands.
Biſhop Fox obtained for him the king's
leave to found, at Baſingſtoke, a free chapel,
and guild of the Holy Ghoſt, the prieſt of
which was to officiate in the chapel, and
teach in the ſchool, which is adjoining.
It was ſuppreſſed in the 37th year of the
ſame reign.

Cardinal Pole, however, reſtored its eſtates, which were again ſeized in the civil
war, but once more reſtored, together with
the ſchool, in 1670, by Biſhop Morley.

The chapel is now in ruins; there remains
only part of the north and ſouth walls, with
a once beautiful hexangular tower, at the
ſouth weſt corner. Of the tomb of its
founder, who was buried here in 1542, not
the ſmalleſt veſtige is now to be diſcovered.
Both the ſchool and the chapel have fallen
into neglect, ſince 1673. The building was
moſt elegantly finiſhed in florid Gothic.

Crossing from Basingstoke, through an open cultivated country, I arrived at Kemp-shot, a hunting-seat of the prince of Wales, which has a small house, and an extensive park. I next passed through Popham-lane, travelling on the old Roman-road from Silchester to Winchester, and through the villages of East-Streton, at which place is the seat of Lord John Russell, and at a short distance are the villages of Kings-Worthy, and Headbourn-Worthy. The country here is pleasantly contrasted, and the eye extends to a view of Winchester, surrounded by lofty hills. On the top of one of these, on the left hand before you enter Winchester, is the chapel of St. Giles, which seems to have been a larger structure than it now appears. At this place, Waldtheof, earl of Northumberland, a noble Saxon, was beheaded, by command of William the Conqueror.

The next place I arrived at was Winchester, the ancient and most famous city of the British Belgæ, called by the Romans

*Venta Belgarum* and *Wintonia*; by the Britons, *Caer Gewent*, and by the Saxons ƿincace ƿceƿ.

It is fituated in a vale, furrounded by lofty hills. The river Itchen paffes the eaft end of the city, where there is a wharf for unlading barges, which come from Southampton, and the parts adjacent. The ftreets in general are narrow, and badly paved, except the high-ftreet, in which ftands the market-crofs, built in the reign of Henry VI. It is a handfome ftructure, richly ornamented, in the Gothic tafte, with figures in niches; but its grandeur has been much diminifhed, by the manner in which it was repaired and painted in 1770, when it was in contemplation to have taken down the whole of this curious memorial of antiquity. This city was confiderable in the time of the Romans; fince it appears, that the emperors had a weaving manufactory here, not only for their own dreffes, and thofe of their army, but alfo for making fail-cloth, and houfehold linen. The emperors breed of Britifh dogs, which were much efteemed, for purpofes of war, as well as for the amufements of the amphitheatre, were trained and kept in this place. Under the Saxon heptarchy, Winchefter was pillaged feveral times; but recovering itfelf after the union of the kingdoms, it became the refidence of the Saxon kings, who embellifhed it with magnificent churches, and made it the fee of a bifhop.

King Ethelftan gave to Winchefter the privilege of having fix mints for the coinage of money. After the Norman conqueft, the city increafed confiderably, and the public records were kept here. The town fuffered confiderably by two accidental fires, and by the licentious violence of the foldiery, during the civil wars between King Stephen and the Emprefs Matilda; the latter proving victorious, made this city her head quarters. But the inhabitants, who were not attached to her caufe, with the affiftance of Henry de Blois, bishop of the fee, betrayed the place into the hands of King Stephen; and Matilda would have been taken prisoner, had she not escaped, by the stratagem of spreading a report that she was dead, and being afterwards carried through the midst of her enemy's army in a coffin.

On the south-side of the west-gate, is an old castle, which sustained many sieges; but the severest was that of 1141, during which, it was defended against King Stephen by the Empress Matilda; when the whole city, with Hyde-abbey, a magnificent and stupendous structure, besides several churches, were burnt by Henry de Blois' adherents, who, having first deserted his brother King Stephen, afterwards took part against the Empress Matilda, and by this conduct, involved the whole kingdom in a civil war. Out of the ruins of Hyde-abbey, the next year, this bishop received from the monks, two hundred and fifteen pounds of silver, and fifteen pounds of gold, besides jewels and other valuables. In this fire perifhed a fuperb crucifix, given by Canute, the Dane, who had expended upon it, as old records fay, one year's revenue of the whole kingdom. It was generally thought, that De Blois took advantage of the times, to get this wealth into his own power, and to humble the monks, whofe abbey was become a rival to the cathedral, which he wifhed to convert into an archbifhoprick for himfelf, and to make the abbey a bifhoprick, dependent upon it. This abbey was originally called *Newanminſtre*, and ftood in the Clofe, hard by St. Swithen's cathedral, which was otherwife called *Ealdenminſtre*.

Thefe abbeys were fo near together, that the voices of the fingers could be heard from one to the other, which occafioned many difputes among the monks, who afterwards proceeded to open quarrels. This circumftance, added to the inconvenience of the air being rendered unwholefome, by the great body of water iffuing from the weft-gate, through the ftreets, and ftagnating at the new monaftery, occafioned Newanmin-ftre to be removed, two hundred years after its foundation, into the fuburb called *Hide*; after which tranflation, it bore the name of Hide-abbey. The bones of Alfred, king of the Weft Saxons, and of Edward, his fon and fucceffor, were brought to this place, and laid in a tomb before the high altar, in which were lately found two fmall tablets of lead, infcribed with their names. There alfo were depofited the bones of St. Grimbald and Judoce.

The building of the caftle is afcribed to King Arthur. Edgar, Edward the Con-feffor, William Rufus, and Richard the Firft, after his return from the holy wars, were crowned here. Sir William Waller took this caftle from King Charles in the civil wars; at which time, it confifted of a fquare ftone building, having a tower at each of the corners. The whole of it was foon afterwards deftroyed, except the Keep, whofe foundation is formed of flint and ftone, and the great hall, where the affizes are now held. In this hall is preferved a large oak-table, which they tell you is King Arthur's celebrated round-table; but it may, with greater propriety, be ftated to have been one of thofe tables, ufed, at an early period, at tournaments or other military feftivals, to prevent difputes of precedence amongft the young nobility.

King Charles the Second began a mag-nificent palace near the fcite of the caftle. It was built, at a great expence, from a defign of Sir Chriftopher Wren. The fhell alone coft £.25,000. The weft-fide of the building is 328 feet long, the fouth-fide 216 feet; and a cupola, of 30 feet high, was intended to have been raifed from the roof, to ferve as a fea-mark. In the original plan was a hand-fome ftreet, formed in a direct line from the palace, to the weft-end of the cathedral; and befides this, a park of ten miles in circum-ference was intended. This palace would

have been fufficiently extenfive to entertain
the whole of the court; and if the fcheme
had been completely carried into execution,
it would have given Winchefter a fuperb
and fplendid appearance, and furnifhed a
lafting memorial of the refined tafte of that
expenfive monarch. During the laft war,
this building was converted into a prifon,
and it is now, by the humanity of the Britifh
Government, made an Afylum for the French
Emigrants.

In this city, it is fuppofed, that King
Lucius founded a monaftery, A.D. 196, and
that the cathedral was begun by Kinegils, the
firft Chriftian King of the Weft Saxons,
after pulling down a college of monks,
which ftood in the heart of the city, in the
time of the Romans, and probably was that
in which Conftans, the monk, refided, before
he was appointed emperor by his father
Conftantine. King Kenwalch finifhed this
cathedral in 646, and the fee of Dorchefter
was transferred hither by Bifhop Wina, in

660. In 963, Bifhop Ethelwold converted this monaftery into a convent of benedictines. The prefent cathedral was begun by Bifhop Walklyn, about the year 1079. He built the tower, the greateft part of the choir, the trancept, and probably the weft-end. The nave was partly repaired by Bifhop Edindon; but William of Wickham, Bifhop of this See, entirely rebuilt it in 1394. The whole of the building, from eaft to weft, is 545 feet, including the chapel of our Lady, which is 54 feet. The choir is 136 feet by 40, the trancept 186 feet long, the centre tower 150 feet high, the nave 300 feet long, and 87 feet wide, including the fide-ailes. The ftalls of the choir were built by Prior Silkftede. The choir under the tower was vaulted in the reign of Charles I. The noble altar-fcreen, the fide-walls, the roof of the prefbytery, and its ailes, were built by Bifhop Fox, in 1525. At the entrance of the choir is a fcreen, defigned by Inigo Jones. Thirteen Saxon kings were buried here, as were alfo King

Lucius, Canute, Hardicanute, William Rufus, Queen Emma, and Richard the Third, fon of William the Conqueror. When the foldiers under Sir William Waller entered this abbey, at the time of the civil wars, they opened the tomb of Rufus, in the choir, and found on his thumb, a gold ring fet with rubies, faid to be worth five hundred pounds. Nor was this the only act of depredation of which they were guilty; for, befides difplacing the bones of the Saxon kings, which had been carefully depofited by Bifhop Fox, in oaken-chefts, richly carved, they damaged feveral of the monuments; and it was with difficulty, that an officer of the name of Cuffe, who had been educated at the college, faved the magnificent tomb of William of Wickham from their fury.

Above twenty Bifhops of Winchefter have been buried in this cathedral. Cardinal Beaufort, Bifhops Edindon, Wainfleet, Wickham, Fox, Gardiner, Langton, Pon-

tiffara, and Toclive, have handfome monuments. The font is a fquare bafon of black
touchftone, adorned with very ancient bas-
reliefs, reprefenting one of the miracles performed by the patron of the church, and is
probably of Saxon antiquity. The cathedral was originally dedicated to St. Swithen.
At the reformation, its eftablifhment was
altered by Henry VIII. to one dean, twelve
prebendaries, fix minor canons, ten lay
clerks, and eight chorifters, with fome inferior officers. He, at the fame time, granted
permiffion to dedicate the cathedral to the
Holy Trinity, fince which period it has been
called Trinity-church. There is alfo a
chapel of the Virgin Mary, and another
called Silkftede's chapel, probably built by
the prior of that name. Over the altar is
a beautiful picture, painted by Mr. Weft,
reprefenting the raifing of Lazarus from the
dead. On the fouth-fide of the cathedral,
ftands the college of St. Mary, founded by
that eminent patron of learning, William
of Wickham, in 1387. The eftablifhment

confifts of a warden, ten fellows, one fchool-
mafter, one ufher, three chaplains, and
feventy fcholars, befides three clerks, and
fixteen chorifters. The building contains
two quadrangles, with a noble chapel, hall,
library, and cloifters, befides a fpacious
quadrangle, contiguous to the college, where
the commoners or fcholars, not on the foundation, live, in a collegiate manner, under the
mafter.

The bifhop's palace, called *Wolvefey*, ftands
oppofite to the college. It is a large building with feveral towers, and has a ftream
running nearly round it. This palace has
undergone a great number of alterations
from the various poffeffors of the See, fo
that fcarcely any part of the original building is left entire.

In this city there was alfo a convent and
abbey, founded by Elfwida, wife of King
Alfred, and dedicated to St. Mary. From this
convent, which, from its ruins appears to

have been very extenfive. From this convent,
Henry I. married Matilda, daughter of Mal-
colm, King of Scotland, the heirefs of the ancient royal family of the Saxons; and thereby
formed an union with the houfe of Normandy.
In Winchefter, there are feveral other buildings of antiquity, but of lefler note, for which
reafon, I fhall pafs them over, and proceed to
fpeak of a ftructure, half a mile fouth of the
town, where ftands the hofpital of St. Crofs,
an ancient and extenfive building. It was
founded by Henry De Blois, in 1136, for
the refidence and maintenance of thirteen
poor men, with provifion for one hundred
others to dine every day. This eftablifhment was altered by Bifhop Toclive in 1185,
and an additional number of penfioners, of
both defcriptions, were added. In 1444,
Cardinal Beaufort alfo gave ample endow-
ments, and greatly increafed the number of
objects. Henry VI. added five hundred
pounds per annum to its revenues, and entitled it the Alms-houfe of Noble Poverty.
Now, however, this well-endowed houfe
maintains only a mafter, nine poor brethren,

and four out-penfioners. The church is a venerable and curious fpecimen of Saxon architecture. It is in the form of a crofs, with ailes; the nave is one hundred and fifty feet long, and the trancept one hundred and twenty.

Leaving St. Crofs, I took the road through Compton, and the pleafant village of Hur-fley. At this place the Bifhop of Win-chefter had formerly a park and caftle, called Merdon, the fcite of which is now a farm. Thefe, together with the village, became the property of Richard, the fon of Oliver Crom-well, in confequence of his marriage with the eldeft daughter of Richard Major, efq. then lord of the manor. Richard Cromwell was buried in the parifh-church, which, with the houfe, was elegantly rebuilt by Sir Wil-liam Heathcote, father of Sir Thomas, the prefent poffeffor. The wood and verdure in this park, are beautiful and luxuriant.

Paffing Otterborne, I proceeded to Stone-ham, the Ad Lapidam of the Ancients.

Here were concealed the two infant brothers of Arvandus, a petty prince of the Isle of Wight, after escaping the massacre on that island. Being betrayed, however, they were at last put to death by order of Ceadwalla. Prior to their execution, Abbot Cymberth, taking pity on their innocence, prevailed on their executioner to let them be baptized at his monastery, at Redford, now called Redbridge.

At North Stoneham, John Fleming, esq. has a handsome house, and extensive park, well stocked with deer. Judiciously placed, on an eminence at the extremity of the latter, stands a summer-house, from which the view is extensive, and well contrasted; and here I first descried the place of my destination, enriched with the prospect of Southampton water and the new forest on the right, whilst, on the left, Portsmouth, Portsea, Gosport, Spithead, bounded with the whole extent of the Isle of Wight, Solent sea, St. Helen's road, the coast of Sussex, and Portsdown hills, were alfo diftinguifhable. I arrived too at a fortunate moment, for the day being fine, and the fun declining, nature was profufe in that variety of beautiful tints, which a lover of the arts fo much admires, together with the view of near four hundred fail of veffels of various defcriptions, rendered the fcene truly picturefque and enchanting.

Farther on the left, is Portfwood-houfe, the feat of General Stibbert, in whofe grounds, on the banks of the Itchen, are the fmall remains of a priory, dedicated to St. Dionyfius. On the oppofite fhore, once a Roman ftation, is Bittern. Near it paffes the Via Icenorum, or Ikelind-ftreet, a Roman way, which extended from Tinmouth, in Northumberland, to Winchefter and Southampton. Before you enter the town, are Bevis Mount (or Padwell) the feat of Edward Horne, efq. and Bellevüe, the refidence of Sir Richard King. Each of thefe, in particular points of view, makes an interefting appearance.

Having travelled twelve miles, I arrived at Southampton, anciently called Hanton, from its fituation on the Tefe, or Anton, and the Arle, or Itchen. The old town is allowed to be the Claufentum of the Romans, which was fituated more eaft, on the ground near St. Mary's church, which ftill retains the ancient privilege of being the mother church of Southampton.

The old town, which had fuffered repeatedly by the ravages of the Danes, at an early period, was at length demolifhed by the French and Genoefe, A.D. 1338, during the conteft between Edward III. and Philip de Valois, for the crown of France. As this ftory may poffibly afford the reader fome amufement, I fhall relate it in the author's words:

" The fourth of October, fiftie galleyes
" well maned and furnifhed came to South-
" ampton, about nine of the clocke, and
" facked the towne, the townfmen running

" away for feare; by the breake of the next
" day they which fled, by the help of the
" country thereabouts came againſt the py-
" rates and fought them, in which ſkirmiſh
" were ſlaine to the number of three hun-
" dred pyrates, together with their captaine,
" a young ſoldiour, the Kinge of Sicilie's
" ſonne: to this young man the French
" Kinge had given whatever he got in the
" kingdome of England; but he being
" beaten down by a certaine man of the
" countrey, cried Rancon: yea (quoth he,
" I know well enough thou art a Francon
" and therefore ſhalt thou dye) for he un-
" derſtood not his ſpeech, neither had he
" any ſkill to take a gentleman priſoner and
" keep them for their ranſome; wherefore
" the riſidue of theſe Gennowayes, after
" they had ſet the towne a fire, and burned
" it quite, fledde to their galleyes; and in
" flying certaine of them was drowned; and
" after this the inhabitants of the towne
" compaſſed it about with a ſtrong and great
" wall."

To preferve the new town, which was
built foon after, from the like calamity, it
was fortified with an embattled wall, built
with ftone, and flanked with towers.  It was
alfo, in many places, fenced by a double
ditch ; and Richard II. in aid of the undertaking, not only granted the inhabitants
feveral of the duties paid at that port, but
alfo built a ftrong caftle, at his own private
expence, for the defence of the harbour.

The prefent town, in point of convenience, is much to be preferred ; as on the
weft and fouth it is wafhed by Southampton
water, and, at a fhort diftance towards the
eaft, by the river Itchen.  It had originally
feven gates, of which fix now remain ; and
the ftrong walls, which once inclofed it, may
yet be traced quite round the town.

Bar-gate, by which you enter the principal ftreet, is not much impaired by time.
Over it, is the town-hall, and the prifon for
debtors.  The ftreet, which is wide, and

well paved, and three quarters of a mile in length, has a ſtriking appearance. Here are good private houſes, and inns, ſhops of every deſcription, and a handſome market houſe, well ſupplied with proviſions three days in the week.

At the end of this ſtreet, is Water-gate, which has been ſtrongly fortified with a port-cullis, and machicolated. This joins the quay, on which ſtands the cuſtom-houſe. Veſſels of conſiderable burthen may unload very commodiouſly. Packets, with the mail for the Iſle of Wight, ſail from this place, every day, except Monday, at ſeven in the morning; and there are boats which go to Portſmouth three times a week. The packet alſo ſails from hence for Jerſey, Guernſey, Alderney, and Sark; a conſiderable trade being carried on with thoſe places, and the merchants having agents at this town, to tranſact their buſineſs. Going to the right when you return from the quay, you paſs God's houſe-gate, and approach South-gate, which is converted into the town-prison. Near this, but much neglected, is a platform of cannon, one of them in several respects curious. It is mounted on a singular kind of carriage, bearing the arms of England and France, quarterly, supported by a griffin and a greyhound, under which is the following inscription.

HENRICUS VIII.
ANGLIE. FRAN
CIE. ET HIBERN
IE. REX FIDEI. DE
FENSOR. INVICT
ISSIMVS. FF.

---

MDXXXII
HR. VIII

---

COLOVRINA. 4 Q 14

Beyond the platform, is a pleasant walk, much frequented in the summer evenings, on account of its delightful situation on the banks of the river Itchen, and under the shade of a double row of trees. The village of *Hithe*, on the other side of Southampton water, and the woods on the opposite shore of the Itchen, are viewed from hence to great advantage. This walk terminates at the ferry, acrofs the Itchen, where Queen Elizabeth built the crofs houfe for the accommodation of paffengers, waiting for the ferry-boat. From this place, you return into the town by Chapel mill. Half a mile farther, at *Northam*, is a large dock-yard, where feveral fhips of war have been built for government by contract. In the fuburb of St. Mary, leading to Eaft-ftreet, there ftood a gate, which bore the fame name, but which has been taken down fome years. It is faid to have been a curious ftructure. Weft Quay gate, which has fuffered much by time, appears to have been once a very ftrong fabric. In the way to it, you pafs the ancient cellars, once ufed for the ftowage of tin, and alum foil, of which great quantities were manufactured at this place; but they are now occupied as warehoufes, for the wool brought from the Ifle of Wight. Henry VI. in the thirty-firft year of his reign, feized on the tin and alum foil, and fold it for his own ufe; allowing, as a compenfation to the merchants, whofe property it legally was, the duties and fole privilege of importing and exporting various articles at the port of Southampton, until they were reimburfed the full value of their goods. Near this fpot, are the affembly rooms and baths, which are commodious, and well adapted for public ufe. In the neighbour- hood too, is another fmall gate, and, on a mount, not far off, where ftood the caftle, which has long been deftroyed, a handfome pleafure-houfe was built, in the year 1741. From the roof of this, every part of the town and adjacent country, may be viewed with fo great advantage, that I would recom- mend every ftranger to vifit it. A fhort time fpent in furveying the furrounding objects, will convey a more correct idea of the place, than can be acquired by any other means.

Southampton contains five churches : St. Lawrence's, Holy Rood, and All Saints, ftand in the high ftreet; St. Michael's is in the fquare, and St. Mary's in the eaft fuburb.

All Saints church is now rebuilding, on a plan which does great honour to the abilities of Mr. Revely, the architect.

A convent of Francifcans or Grey Friars, was founded here, A.D. 1240. This order originated in the penitentiary facrifices of a debauched youth, of the name of Francis, who was born at Aſſiſy, in Umbria, and who was diſinherited for robbing his father. Stung with remorſe, however, for the profligacy of his life, he retired, in the year 1206, to a little chapel, near Aſſiſy, called Our Lady of the Angels. Here he led ſo rigid a life, that, in a ſhort time, he attracted many admirers, and at laſt followers and companions, of whom he made himſelf the head, and formed a ſet of rules, for the regulation of this order, which, in a ſhort time, became a very numerous body.

Near this, is God's houſe, a very ancient eſtabliſhment, founded by Roger Hampton. The deed, which is in the archives of the corporation, is so decayed by time, that the date cannot be made out. By a charter of Edward III. however, it was granted to Queen's college, Oxford, with a proviso, that, out of the rents, a fund should be formed for the maintenance of such poor scholars of the college, as had the misfortune to labour under incurable diforders. God's houfe, at prefent, confifts of a warden, four old men, and the fame number of women, who each have an allowance of two shillings a week, and lodging.

In the chapel of St. Julian at this place, were interred the bodies of Richard Earl of Cambridge, Sir Thomas Grey, and Lord Scrope, after their execution, for a conspiracy against the life of Henry V. when he was preparing to embark for France. To carry on this defign, it is faid, the fum of one million, in gold, was remitted them from France. They were greatly in the king's confidence, but the Earl of March, one of the conspirators, forefeeing the confequences which would follow to the nation if this bloody tranſaction were accompliſhed, revealed the whole plot. Earl Cambridge and Sir Thomas Grey were beheaded, and Lord Scrope was hanged, drawn, and quartered.

Southampton contains ſeveral other public foundations, which it is unneceſſary to deſcribe minutely. On the ſhore, it is ſaid, Canute the Great, wiſely reproved the flattery of his courtiers, who ſervilely endeavoured to perſuade him, that all nature, even the waves of the ſea, muſt obey his mandate.

Domeſday-book ſtates, that in the year 1080, Southampton had but eighty men, tenants in demeſne. Either the ruinous condition in which it was left by the Danes, or the ſubſequent impediments to its re-eſtabliſhment, muſt have occaſioned this. However, when the nation was more ſettled, the inhabitants applied to commerce, and their firſt objeſt was to be incorporated, or, as it was then called, to be made a Guild, by which certain liberties, exclufive privileges and immunities were fecured to them.

Their firft charter was granted by Henry II. and it was afterwards confirmed by Richard I. King John, Edward III. and Richard II. But Henry IV. extended their privileges ftill farther, and thefe were confirmed to them by Henry V. and VI.

To Southampton belonged the fole privilege of importing canary wines, which the inhabitants even fupplied to the merchants of the metropolis. It alfo ranked next to the port of London, in the importation of other wines.

According to the laft charter which was granted by Charles I. though only a confirmation of former charters, the corporation is directed to confift of a mayor, recorder, fheriff, and two bailiffs. Perfons who have ferved any of thofe offices become members of the common council, which is un-limited with refpect to number. The cor-poration have a power of choofing burgeffes, who, though not members of the common council, are yet of the corporation, and have votes. There are eleven juftices of the peace, to wit, the mayor, the bifhop of Winchefter, the recorder, the laft mayor for the time being, five aldermen, and two bur-geffes. All who have paffed the chair are aldermen, and befides thofe already men-tioned, there are feveral officers, fuch as the town clerk, four ferjeants at mace, a town crier, &c.

This borough was made a county in it-felf, independent of the lord lieutenant and fheriff of the fhire, by Henry II. and this right was confirmed by King John and his fucceffors.

It returns to parliament two members, who are elected by the inhabitants paying fcot and lot. The mayor is admiral of the liberties from South Sea Caſtle to Hurſt Caſtle.

Since the year 1067, Southampton has given the title of Earl to the families of Beauvois, Fitzwilliams, and Wriotheſley; but in 1675, Charles Fitzroy, eldeſt natural ſon of King Charles II. by the Duchefs of Cleveland, was created Duke of Southampton. At preſent the title of Lord Southampton exiſts in the perſon of Charles Fitzroy, a relation of the Duke of Grafton, created a Baron, in 1780, by his preſent Majeſty.

Of this place nothing farther need be ſaid, than that it ſupplies every kind of accommodation and amuſement, both for valetudinarians and the faſhionable world. The environs of the town and the unfiniſhed Polygon, are pleaſant and airy. The country abounds with deſirable walks, and the means of a variety of pleaſing excurſions on horſeback, or in boats on the water, offer to

ftrangers an agreeable change of amufements.

After having feen every thing worthy of
notice at Southampton, I determined on
vifiting, in my way to the ifland, the ruins
of Netley Abbey; and as I had already made
my obfervations on the oppofite fhore of
Southampton water, I ordered a boat to wait
for me at the Abbey fort, which is three
miles diftant from Southampton, and purfued the foot path to thofe celebrated ruins.

The road down Eaft-ftreet, leads to Itchen-
ferry. On the oppofite fide of the river
ftands the village of Itchen, confifting of a
few houfes, chiefly inhabited by fifhermen.
I took the right hand path, through a copfe
of confiderable length, which occafionally
affords different views of Southampton, at
the different openings formed by the hand
of nature. Thefe varieties of profpect are
extremely interefting, and would afford many
beautiful fubjects for the pencil.

Drawn & Engraved by Cha⁻ Heathcote

Published as the Act Directs by C and G Kearsley, Fleet Street 1799

On leaving the copfe, I croffed feveral
fields, through an agreeable ferpentine path,
which brought me to the lawn of Woolfon-
houfe, one of the feats of N. Dance, Efq.
R. A. the proprietor of the eftate of which
Netley-Abbey forms a part. From hence,
I defcended a fmall hill, through the adjoining fields, which are enlivened with a
view of the New-Foreft and Southampton
water, until I came to the rural village of
Wefton. I then paffed acrofs feveral meadows, which terminate in an extenfive wood,
through which the path is continued for upwards of a mile, winding in various directions. Towards the end of it, the foliage
thickens confiderably, and renders the weft
end of Netley-Abbey, which here firft ftrikes
the eye of the vifitor of this charmingly
fecluded edifice, extremely picturefque.

The remains of this Abbey are fituated in
a dell, furrounded with various trees, which
greatly relieve the building, and add much
to its antiquated fplendour. The path, by

an eafy defcent to the left, leads towards the outer gate, which is kept locked to prevent depredations. Mr. Dance's keeper has a fmall houfe, about a quarter of a mile from the Abbey, where refrefhments are provided; or his family will wait on thofe parties who bring provifions for themfelves, and wifh to regale under the fhadow of thefe magnificent ruins, which is very frequently done. On entering the outer gate, I croffed the fpace formerly occupied by the porter of the Abbey, and paffed through a fmaller gate, into a fpacious cloifter court. Here, a number of afh trees, which appear to have grown fpontaneoufly, affift greatly in producing that gloomy ftillnefs fo highly grateful to the minds of all, who contemplate thefe once facred abodes of religion and folitude.

On the left of the cloifter court, are feveral doors, which lead to fmall apartments. On the right fide, there are likewife doors, leading to the chapel and the habitable parts of

Drawn & Engraved by Edwd Dayes

Published as the Act directs by Edwd G. Hearsley Hatton Street 1794

the building. Paffing through feveral fquare
apartments, I was fhewn a large vaulted
room, which is called the Abbot's kitchen;
but from its dark and gloomy appearance,
I fhould rather fuppofe it to have been one
of the cellars belonging to the Abbey. There
is yet remaining in the fouth aile, a part of
the ftone cieling, in which are feveral coats of
arms, neatly carved, and in a good ftate of
prefervation. Thefe, and the different orna-
ments fcattered about, fhow that the work-
manfhip of the building was fuperb and
well executed. The ftone is of a clofe texture
and exceedingly firm, and in many parts it
has the appearance of having been lately cut.

Of the eaft window, which is large and
handfome, fome judgment may be formed
from the annexed view; but the fcale of this
work is much too fmall to do juftice to fo
noble a fubject.

If the trees in the infide of the chapel were
thinned with judgment, it would give fome-

what more confequence to the ruins, and preferve them alfo from the damp, which fo
large a quantity of furrounding foliage com-
municates.

A fmall ftair-cafe ftill remains, by which
you may afcend to the top of the building,
and view the ruins to great advantage.

Here the ivy is luxuriant and picturefque,
and the body of the chapel is feen filled with
fragments of the building, overgrown with
weeds and mofs.

" From the rent roof and portico fublime,
Where rev'rend fhrines in gothic grandeur ftood,
The nettle or the noxious nightfhade fpreads ;
And afhlings, wafted from the neighbouring wood,
Through the worn turret wave their trembling heads."

Necteleye, Lettley, Netley, or Edward-
ftow, is pleafantly fituated in the parifh of
Hound, on the eaftern banks of Southampton water, three miles below the town.
Leland and Godwin attribute the founding

of the Abbey to Peter de Rupibus, who
died in 1238. But Dugdale and Tanner differ from them in opinion. Thofe learned anti-
quaries fay, that an Abbey for Ciftertian monks
from Beaulieu, dedicated to St. Mary and
St. Edward, was founded by Henry III. A.D.
1239, which probably was this very edifice, as
the fituation perfectly agrees with the place
where the king is faid to have built it. On
the fuppreffion of this monaftery, it was occupied by an abbot and twelve monks, whofe
poffeffions were valued, according to Dugdale, at £.100 12s. 8d. but according to
Speed, at £.160 2s. 9d.

The order of Ciftertian Monks was originally founded by Robert, Abbot of
Molfme, who, being tired of the diffolute
life which the monks of that monaftery
led, withdrew himfelf, with twenty-one of
his religious companions, into the folitudes
of Citeaux, five leagues diftant from the
city of Dijon, in Burgundy. Oto I. Duke of
Burgundy, endowed this eftablifhment with

confiderable revenues. The monks followed the rule of St. Bennet, with the addition of fome conftitutions, framed with the confent of his brethren, by Stephen III. abbot of this order, and confirmed, in 1107, by Pope Urban II. This order exifted in England before the year 1132, as, at that time, they had a monaftery at Rifhval. Their habit was originally black, but it was changed by Barnard, one of their abbots, who pretended, that the Virgin Mary appeared to him, and commanded him, for her fake, to wear white clothes.

At the reformation, Henry VIII. granted this Abbey and its poffeffions to Sir William Paulet. About the middle of the fixteenth century, it was the feat of the Earl of Hereford, and was afterwards fitted up and inhabited by the Marquis of Huntingdon, who, it is faid, converted the weft end of the chapel into a kitchen and other offices, referving the eaft end for facred purpofes. In the year 1700, it came into the poffeffion of

Sir Bartlet Lucy, who fold the materials of the chapel to one Taylor, a carpenter of Southampton, who took off the roof, which, till then, had remained entire. The fate of this artificer, as related by Brown Willis, in his Hiftory of Mitred Abbeys, I fhall introduce here, as I found, upon enquiring of fome of his family, who are now living at Southampton, that the account is a true one :

" During the time that Walter Taylor
" was in treaty with Sir Bartlet Lucy, he
" was greatly difturbed by frightful dreams,
" as fome fay, apparitions, particularly by
" that of a perfon in the habit of a monk,
" who threatened him with great mifchief if
" he perfifted in his purpofe : one night in
" particular, he dreamed a large ftone from
" one of the windows fell upon him and
" killed him. This fo terrified him, that he
" communicated thefe difturbances to a par-
" ticular friend, who advifed him to defift ;
" but avarice and the contrary advice of

" other friends, getting the better of his
" fears, he concluded the bargain, when, at—
" tempting to take out some stones from
" the bottom of the west wall, the whole
" body of a window fell upon him and
" crushed him to death."

The ruins of Netley-abbey became after—
wards the property of Henry Cliff, esq. who
sold them to the late Mr. Dummer. They
are now in the possession of N. Dance, esq.
R.A. who married Mr. Dummer's widow.
At some distance from the building, to the
eastward, there are large mounds, which appear to have been the heads of fish-ponds
or reservoirs for fresh water, the tide of
Southampton water being salt. A little to
the westward, on the shore of Southampton
water, stands a ruined castle, the shell of
which now only remains. From its con—
struction, it appears to have been built con—
siderably later than the abbey. This ruin
consists of a square centre building, which
you enter by a flight of steps, through a

Published as the Act Directs, Apl 1 1787 by Boulsby Stockton bear bow 1784

Drawn & Engraved by J.D. Staircase

fmall door, that appears to have had a port-
cullis on the eaft-fide. It has likewife been
defended with a deep moat, a double platform for cannon, and a wing on each fide,
of nearly the fame dimenfions as the centre,
with battlements on the top.

Leaving this place, I reached the fhore of
Southampton water, at the Abbey-fort, of
the ftructure and fituation of which, the
annexed fketch, taken with a view towards
Southampton, will give the reader an idea.

The tide and a gentle breeze being in my
favour, I went into the boat, and paffed
Gatlands, a feat of Mr. Drummond, the
fituation of which is extremely pleafant;
the new foreft adorning the right hand fhore,
with a variegated and rich fcenery. On a
hill upon the left hand, ftands Hamble-
church, a plain building, with a fquare
tower, which ferves as a land-mark. Mrs.
York, is building a handfome houfe on
the fhore, not very diftant from that part

of the Hamble-river, which joins Southampton water.

Moored at the mouth of this river, is a
handſome veſſel, the property of Governor
Hornby, who has an elegant houſe, in the
pariſh of Hook, at the extreme point of
land on the left of the mouth of Southampton water, which, in this part, is about
two miles acroſs.   Nearly oppoſite to Hook,
I ſtopped to take a drawing of Calſhot-
caſtle, and a diſtant proſpect of the Iſle of
Wight, which form the fourth view in this
work.   I afterwards landed to ſee the caſtle,
which is ſituated on a neck of land projecting into the Solent ſea, at the entrance of
Southampton water.   It was built in the
reign of Henry VIII. for the defence of this
part of the coaſt and Southampton harbour.
The platform, where the large cannon are
mounted, is a polygon, ſurrounded by a
moat, the upper part, which is at preſent
fitted up for the officer, is circular.   From
the top of it, I had an extenſive view to the

eaft and weft, and alfo of the whole extent
of the Ifle of Wight, which appears to great
advantage.

Taking water again, I approached the
Brambles, a fand-bank which runs nearly
up to Spithead. Here the mafts of a collier,
which was bound to Southampton, and loft
on thefe fands, are ftill feen.

> " Now favour'd with a mild propitious gale,
> We to the breeze expand the fwelling fail;
> The land recedes—the veffel feems to fleep,
> Smooth, gliding o'er the furface of the deep;
> Near, and more near, advancing Veſta moves,
> Along her fhores the eye delighted roves;
> Secure from ftorms, here lies the circling bay,
> Fair rural views afcending from the fea;
> There lowering rocks a threat'ning ruin fhow,
> And here the dafhing furges rage below."

Approaching the fhore, Cowes-harbour
and the village make a ftriking appearance,
the houfes being built in irregular ranges
above each other, on a rifing ground, in-
termixed with gardens and lofty trees.

Covering the oppofite fhore of the Medina,
is the village of Eaft-Cowes, at which place,
all the cuftom-houfe duties are paid, for the
fhips that arrive in the harbour. On the
high ground above the village, Mr. Aljoe has
built a houfe, the profpect from which, to
the weftward, is very extenfive. The village
of Eaft Cowes, the River Medina, and Weft-
Còwes, form agreeable and bufy fcenes, enlivened ftill more by the veffels continually
paffing, and the boats from the fhipping,
which lie at anchor in Cowes-road. This
place is the general refort of foreign veffels,
owing to the convenience of the fituation
and tides, which enable them to turn out
either to the eaftward or weftward, without
difficulty.

After two hours failing, I arrived at Weft-
Cowes, a village confifting of one ftreet,
chiefly inhabited by tradefmen, who fupply
the fhipping that arrive, with any article
they may want. At this place, there is a
private dock-yard, which, within the laft

COWES HARBOUR.

Drawn in England by Tho...

...commuted in Strstrais by Gred & Academy Feb. 1801 1794

fixty years, has contributed to the Britifh navy, the following fhips of war, namely, the Vanguard of feventy guns, the Repulfe of fixty-four, the Salifbury of fifty, the Cerberus and Aftrea of thirty-two, the Andromeda of twenty-eight, the Veteran of fixtyfour guns, and the Experiment of forty-four; befides a number of fmaller veffels.

The chief imports of the Ifland, are timber, deals, and iron. Thefe articles, which are deftined for Dorfetfhire, and Suffex, are landed at this port, on account of its accommodation for loading and unloading. Of late years, confiderable quantities of wine, fome cargoes of hemp, and alfo fruits from Spain and Portugal, have been configned hither. Before the feparation of the American colonies from Great-Britain, there annually arrived from Georgia and South Carolina, a number of veffels laden with rice, whofe cargoes were computed at thirty or forty thoufand barrels. The rice was landed, opened, fkreened, and repacked; and

generally fhipped again for Holland, Germany, or fome of the French ports. Thefe
fhips likewife brought tobacco, deer-fkins,
ftaves, indigo, pitch, tar, and various other
articles. Since the eftablifhment of the in-
dependence of America, the port of Cowes
has been deprived of the advantages of thefe
beneficial imports. The articles exported
from the Ifland, confift of wheat, flour, malt,
barley, wool, and falt ; of which large quantities are fhipped for France, Spain, Portugal,
and the ports in the Mediterranean.

There are two inns at Weft-Cowes, and
a number of lodging-houfes, for the accommodation of ftrangers, who, of late years,
have frequented it as a bathing-place, in
which refpect, befides the conveniences common for fea bathing, it poffeffes the fingular
advantage of a fhore, on which parties may
bathe at any ftate of the tide.

Cowes-caftle, which ftands near the bathing
place, was built by Henry VIII. as a pro-

COWES CASTLE.

tection to the port. It confifts of a fmall
battery, in the form of a crefcent, which
mounts a few cannon. The circular tower
and fquare building, are occupied by the
officer and gunner. In the upper part of
this town, are feveral neat houfes, inhabited
by different gentlemen, which poffefs great
advantages in point of profpect. One of
thefe on the fea-fhore, called *Egypt*, is a delightful fummer refidence.

This Ifland, known to us by the name of
the Ifle of *Wight*, was called by the Britons,
*Guith*; by the Romans, Vecta, or Vectis, and
by the Saxons, ꝑitlanꝺ, and Ƿicp-Ꞃa. This, which
is the largeft and moft valuable of the appen-
dant Britifh Iflands, is fituated oppofite the
fouth coaft of England, from which it is
feparated by a channel, varying in breadth,
from one mile to feven, formerly called the
Solent Sea. It forms a part of the county
of Southampton, or Hampfhire, and is within the Diocefe of Winchefter. The figure

of the Ifland, is an irregular lozenge ; in length from eaft to weft, upwards of twenty-two miles, and in breadth, from north to fouth, in the wideft part, near fourteen miles. It is reckoned to contain a hundred and thirty thoufand acres of land, and poffeffes every variety of foil that can be found in any other part of Great-Britain. Its fertility is fo remarkable, that it has been faid to produce, in one year, enough to fupply the confumption of its inhabitants, for eight years ; but the prefent produce, from the many improvements which have been made in agriculture, muft confiderably exceed the former computation. Extending from the eaft to the weft end of the Ifland, we fee a range of downs, from feveral parts of which, particularly Afhey, Bucombe, and St. Catharine's, nearly the whole coaft of the Ifland may be feen, together with the adjacent fhores of Dorfetfhire, Hampfhire, and Suffex. Thefe downs afford excellent pafture for fheep, of which there are great numbers bred in the

Ifland. The lambs are fent to different markets, and fome thoufands are annually carried to London. Their wool, which is fcarcely inferior to that of Leominfter, and Cotfwold, fupplies the different cloathing towns in Dorfetfhire and Devonfhire, with many thoufand tods yearly, and is fold in the fleece. Every fpecies of fifh that is found on the Englifh coafts is caught here, and the fouthern fide of the Ifland abounds with fuch plenty of fhell-fifh, that a village has obtained the name of *Crab* Niton, from the abundance of crabs which are caught near it.

Some years back, this place was well furnifhed with game of all forts, but it has been much thinned of late, by the great number of fportfmen that have traverfed the Ifland for their amufement. It has been remarked, however, that there is neither fox, badger, nor pole-cat, to affift in their deftruction. In the months of May, June, July, and Auguft, great numbers of fea birds affemble to take

advantage of the folar rays, on the fouth-
fide of the Ifland, to breed up their young.
Poultry of every denomination is bred here,
to the great accommodation of the veffels
anchoring at the different ports, and at St.
Helen's, and the Mother Bank.

Formerly, there was plenty of timber upon
the Ifland ; but being fituated fo near to
Portfmouth dock-yard, the confumption of
that place and of its own private yards, for
fhip building, has reduced it to a quantity
fcarcely fufficient for private confumption.
The water, of which there are various fprings
equal in purity to that of Briftol, I have been
informed, has frequently undergone the experiment of a Weft-India voyage, and returned in a pure and wholefome ftate.

The prefent divifion of the Ifle of Wight,
is into two hundreds, feparated by the
courfe of the River Mede, Medham, or, as
it is now called, Medina, which rifing near

the bottom of St. Catharine's down, runs northward, and discharges itself into the channel, between East and West Cowes. These hundreds are distinguished by the names of East and West Medina, according to their situation in respect to that River. Formerly the east was called Hommerswell, and the west, Bowcomb hundred. In Doomsday-book, mention is made of a third hundred, lying in that of Bowcomb, and called Cauborn hundred; probably on account of its belonging to the fee of Winchester, and thence enjoying peculiar immunities. The Island at present contains thirty parishes, some of which are small, and have obtained the denomination of separate parishes, merely from having distinct parochial rates. The following is a list of the names of the parishes as they are situated in the two hundreds.

| *Eaſt Medina.* | *Weſt Medina.* |
|---|---|
| Arreton | Brixton |
| Binſtead | Brook |
| Bonechurch | Calborne |
| Brading | Chale |
| Godſhill | Cariſbrook |
| Newchurch | Freſhwater |
| Niton | Gatcombe |
| Shanklin | Kingſton |
| St. Helen's | Mottiſton |
| St. Laurence | Newport |
| Whippingham | Northwood |
| Whitwell | St. Nicholas |
| Wootton | Shorwell |
| Yaveland | Shalfleet |
|  | Thorley |
|  | Yarmouth. |

According to the beſt information I can colleſt, the inhabitants are about twenty thouſand in number. The population has therefore increafed confiderably fince the year 1377, when the number was afcertained to be no more than feven thoufand and ninety-nine. The inhabitants cannot be fuppofed to differ from thofe of the adjacent country, the diftance being too fmall to caufe any variation, and the conftant intercourfe with the metropolis having erafed all the infular peculiarities that might have exifted formerly. Their hofpitality ftands unrivalled ; and indeed no part of Great Britain can boaft a more univerfal exercife of the focial virtues than this Ifland, which feems highly favoured by nature in every refpect.

> " Nor, Vecta, be thy generous fons unfung,
> To whom the manly graces all belong ;
> Courage to act and prudence to controul,
> The focial temper, and the friendly foul ;
> Their language pure, their fentiments refin'd,
> Nor lefs complete in perfon than in mind ;
> Of comely fize ; to health, to vigour known ;
> Untainted with the vices of the Town.
> View in thy daughters fair proportion rife,
> The fnowy bofom, and the fparkling eyes ;

And midft the bloom of beauty and of youth,
Mild modeft virtue, and unfullied truth ;
With ev'ry grace adorn'd and namelefs art
To charm the fenfe, and captivate the heart ;
Loves round them fport, in innocence they fmile,
And crown the glories of the happy Ifle."

The Ifle of Wight has been ftated, by various writers of eminence, to have formerly joined the main land of Great Britain, and to have been gradually disjoined by the encroachments of the fea, which is there called the Solent, or more properly the *Solvent* fea, from the Latin verb *folvere*, to loofen or fet at liberty. To give the reader as correct an idea of every thing relative to this Ifland as poffible, I fhall introduce the opinions of two very ingenious writers on this fubject.

Mr. Borlafe, in his Natural Hiftory of Cornwall, expreffes his fentiments concerning the Ifle of Wight in the following argument- " The fhort defcription which we have of the tin trade in Diodorus Siculus, muft not be omitted, though it is too general for us to learn many particulars from it. Thefe men, (fays he, meaning the tinners), manufacture their tin, by working the grounds, which produce it, with great art; for though the land is rocky, it has foft veins of earth running through it, in which the tinners find the treafure, extract, melt and purify it; then fhaping it, by moulds, into a kind of cubical figure, they carry it off to a certain Ifland, lying near the Britifh fhore, which they call Ictis. For at the recefs of the tide, the fpace betwixt the Ifland and the main land being dry, the tinners embrace the opportunity, and carry the tin in carts, as faft as may be, over to the Ictis or port; for it muft be obferved, that the Iflands which lie betwixt the Continent and Britain have this fingularity, that when the tide is full they are real Iflands, but when the fea retires they are all but fo many peninfulas. From this Ifland the merchants buy their tin of the natives, and export it into Gaul, and finally through Gaul, by a journey of about thirty days, they bring it down on horſes, to the mouth of the Erydanus, meaning the Rhone. In this deſcription it will naturally occur to the inquiſitive reader, to aſk where this Iĉtis was, to which the Corniſh carried their melted tin in carts, and there ſold it to the merchants. I really cannot inform him; but by the Iĉtis here, it is plain, that the hiſ-torian could not mean the Iĉtis or Veĉtis of the Ancients, at preſent called the Iſle of Wight: for he is ſpeaking of the Britons of Cornwall, and, by the words, it ſhould ſeem thoſe of the moſt weſtern parts ; Της ναρ Βρεία-νικης καία το ακρωίηρου το καλυμενον Βελεριον οι μαίοικυν-ίες, &c. Ουίοι τον κοσσίερον καίασκευαζυσι Φιλοίεχνας, &c. that is, thoſe who live at the ex-treme end of Britain, called Belerium, (now called the Lands’ End,) find, dreſs, melt, carry, and ſell their tin, &c. Now it would be abſurd to think theſe inhabitants ſhould carry in carts their tin, nearly two hundred miles, for ſo diſtant is the Iſle of Wight from them, when they had at leaſt as good ports and harbours on their own ſhores, as they

could meet with there; befides, the inhabitants are faid in the fame paragraph, to have
been more than ordinarily civilized by con-
verfing with ftrangers and merchants. Thofe
merchants then muft have been very con-
verfant in Cornwall; there trafficked for tin,
that is there bought, and thence exported
the tin, or they could have no bufinefs there:
their refidence would have been in fome of
the ports of Hampfhire, and Cornwall would
fcarce have felt the influence of their man-
ners, much lefs have been improved and
civilized by them at that diftance. Again,
the Cornifh, after the tin was melted, carried
it, at low water, over the Ictis, in carts; this
will by no means fuit the fituation of the
Ifle of Wight, which is at leaft two miles
diftant from the main land; and never, fo
far as we can learn, has been alternately an
ifland and a peninfula, as the tide is in and
out. The Ictis, therefore, here mentioned,
muft lie fomewhere near the coaft of Cornwall; and muft either have been a general
name for any peninfula or creek, (*Ik* being

a common Cornifh word, denoting a cove,
creek, or port of traffick), or the name of
fome particular peninfula and common
emporium on the fame coaft, which has now
loft its ifthmus, name, and perhaps wholly
difappeared, by means of fome great alterations on the fea fhore of this country."
The opinion of Mr. Whitaker differs much
from this. In his Hiftory of Manchefter, after mentioning that the Phœnicians had continued the tin trade on the coafts of Scilly
for three hundred years, fays " The Greeks
of Marfeilles, firft followed the track of the
Phœnician voyagers, and before the days of
Polybius, and about two hundred years before the age of Chrift, began to fhare with
them in the trade of tin. The Cartha-
ginian commerce declined.——The Maffylian
commerce increafed; and in the reign of
Auguftus, the whole current of the Britifh
traffick had been gradually diverted into this
channel. Two roads were laid acrofs the
country, and reached from Sandwich to Car-

narvon on the one fide, and extended from
Dorfetfhire into Suffolk on the other. The
great Staple of tin was no longer fettled in
a diftant corner of the Ifland. It was removed from Scilly, and was fixed at the Ifle
of Wight, a central part of the coaft, lying
equally betwixt the two roads, and better
adapted to the new arrangement of the
trade. Thither the tin was carried by the
Belgæ, and thither the foreign merchants
reforted with their wares." He adds further,
" that the Ifle of Wight, which, as late as
the eighth century, was feparated from the remainder of Hampfhire by a channel no lefs
than three miles in breadth, was now actually
a part of the greater Ifland; disjoined from
it only by the tide, and united to it always at
the ebb. And during the recefs of the waters,
the Britons conftantly paffed over the low
ifthmus of land, and carried their loaded
carts of tin acrofs it."

A gentleman of the ifland, in fupport of
Mr. Whitaker's opinion, has remarked, that

at each extremity of the channel, between the ifland and Hampfhire, the tide rufhes in and out with fuch impetuofity, as to render thefe parts the deepeft and moft dangerous; but in the midway, where the tides meet, though the conflict occafions rough water, according as the wind may happen to affift the one or the other, there is no rapidity of current to carry away the foil and deepen the bottom. Nearly acrofs the channel, a gravelly beach extends, which is only found in this part and on the oppofite fhore of Hampfhire, at a place called Leap. This probably was the narrow pafs before alluded to, and along which, the Cornifh men tranfported their tin to the Ifle of Wight.

Oppofite to this place, is a ftraight open road above two miles in length, called Rew Street. This road runs quite acrofs the foreft of Parkhurft, and may be eafily traced to the weft of Carifbrook caftle, over a field called North-Field, by Sheat, and from thence to the South part of the ifland. No ufe is at prefent made of many parts of this road, and unlefs it was efpecially made for the convey-ance of the tin, it is not eafy to conceive what purpofe it was to anfwer. To prove that the Staple of tin was brought into Hampfhire, there is undoubted authority; but, that a port on the South fide of the ifland, to which this road is fuppofed to lead, was the place from whence the tin was exported, is a fup-pofition that wants confirmation. No part of the South coaft of the ifland feems adapted for a fea port, and the fact is ftill more to be doubted when we reflect on the convenience of the port of Southampton for that purpofe; for furely our anceftors muft have known their own intereft and convenience better than to have given themfelves unneceffary trouble in conveying fo ponderous an article by land, without deriving any particular advantage from that mode. It is alfo known, that the office of the Stannaries, was not removed from Southampton till the fif-teenth century.

The Ifle of Wight not having been under any other government than that of Britain, has therefore no feparate hiftory of its own. As connected with the Hiftory of England indeed, we find this ifland mentioned occafionally in the Roman, Saxon, and other annals, of the ancient fituation of the country; but the accounts are few and unconnected: whole centuries fometimes intervening, without any mention being made of it. For the fatisfaction of our readers, however, we fhall give a detail of fuch particulars as we have been able to collect from the fcattered relics of antiquity, and in the order of time in which they occurred.

Very little is known of the hiftory of Britain before the landing of Julius Cæfar, about fifty-five years before the birth of Chrift; nor have we any account of the Romans having entered the Ifle of Wight, until near a century afterwards, when Claudius, the Emperor of Rome, in the year 43, fent an army into Britain under Plautius, who, after various fucceffes againft Togodumnus and Caractacus, two kings of Britain, was recalled to Rome, and received the honour of an oration or inferior triumph, has the reward of his fervices. Tacitus, in his Life of Agricola, informs us, that Plautius fought thirty battles with the Britons, fubdued two powerful nations, and conquered the Ifle of Wight. We are not told of any oppofition that Plautius met with in the ifland, nor indeed is it to be fuppofed that the inhabitants were capable of any effectual refiftance to the powerful and victorious legions of Rome, who, moft probably, entered the ifland without any difficulty, from the Hampfhire coaft, after having fubdued that county. And this conjecture is the more probable, as no appearances exift, in any part of the ifland, of thofe fortified camps in which the Romans never failed to fecure themfelves, when they had an enemy oppofed to them, and which are to be found in fo many other parts of England.

The dominion of the Romans over Britain, continued from this period till about the year 426; and it is probable, that during that space of time, the Isle of Wight remained peaceably under their subjection.

For more than twenty years after the Romans withdrew themselves, the Britons were continually harrassed by the Picts and Scots, who coming from the Northern part of the island, do not, however, appear to have penetrated so far as the Isle of Wight. At length, the Britons, having invited the Saxons to assist them against the Northern depredators, the latter began also to settle in Britain, and formed several kingdoms for themselves.

In 495, Cerdic, a Saxon General, arrived in Britain. He landed with his son Cenric, at a place which was thence called *Cerdic's Ora,* which Camden supposes to have been Yarmouth, in Norfolk; but some other authors imagine it to have been near Southampton; and Gibſon, in his Gloſſary, at the end of the Saxon Annals, with great appearance of probability, ſtates it to have been Calſhot, of which we have already ſpoken.

After a variety of alternate ſucceſſes and defeats, Cerdic, in the year 519, gained a great victory over the Britons under Auther, one of their leaders, at a place called by the Saxons, *Cerdic's-ford*, (now Chardford) in Hampſhire, where he had before defeated the Britons in 508. In conſequence of thi victory, the counties of Hampſhire and Somerſetſhire were ſurrendered to Cerdic, who formed, of them, the kingdom of Weſſex, to which, in the year 828, the reſt of the kingdoms of the Saxon Heptarchy were ſubjected.

In 530, Cerdic having attacked and ſubdued the Iſle of Wight, deſtroyed the greateſt part of the inhabitants; and having invited over from Germany a conſiderable number of Saxons and Jules, he diſtributed a great part of the latter through this ifland, the government of which he conferred on his nephews Stuff and Withgar, who had brought him a confiderable reinforcement from the Continent in the year 514, and ferved him with great fidelity fince his laft victory at Cerdic's-ford, to which they had themfelves been very inftrumental.

Withgar, in all probability, continued in the government of the ifland till his death, as he was buried in the town, which was named from him *Withgaraburgh*, and is now, by contraction, called Carifbrook.

Wulfer, who fucceeded his father Penda in the kingdom of Mereia, in 659, took the Ifle of Wight from Cenowalch, king of Weffex; and about the year 661, made a prefent of it to Adelwalch, king of Suffex, whom he had fubdued and held in captivity.

In 686, Cedwalla, king of Weffex, attacked the Ifle of Wight, which had been in the poffeffion of the kings of Suffex from the time it had been granted to Adelwalch by Wulfer; and though it was defended by the Governor Arwald, brother of Auther, king of Suffex, Cedwalla took it by the fuperiority of his forces.

Upon the firft impulfe of his zeal for religion, Cedwalla determined to exterminate the inhabitants of the ifland who had not embraced Chriftianity, and to people it with Chriftians; but in confequence of the humane advice of Widfrid, Bifhop of Selfey, in Suffex, he was induced to fpare the lives of fuch of them as would confent to be baptized immediately. Birwin, nephew of Widfred, was fent into the ifland to convert the inhabitants, who, wifely preferring the Chriftian Religion to death, ceafed from that time to be idolaters. In how many inftances, in the hiftory of all countries, have the capricious inclinations and opinions of Princes been the occafion of a change in Religion !

It is faid, that, in the reign of Alfred, a fleet of Danifh pirates plundered the Ifle of Wight. In the fucceeding reign, of Ethelred II. the Danes again made themfelves mafters of it, as well as of Hampfhire and Dorfetfhire. In thefe places they kept their magazines, and from thence they made frequent excurfions into the adjoining counties, which they ravaged without oppofition.

During the reign of Edward the Confeffor, in 1052, Earl Godwin, being banifhed by the king, retired to Flanders, where, having obtained fome fhips from the Earl of that country, he made a defcent on the Ifle of Wight, and extorted very large fums of money from the inhabitants, whilft he was waiting there for his fon Harold.

In 1066, Tofton, or Tofti, Earl of Northumberland, having been driven out of that county, procured feveral fhips from the fame Earl of Flanders, who was his father-in-law. With thefe he infefted the Englifh coaft for fome time, and plundered the Ifle of Wight.

For a confiderable length of time after this took place, the ifland appears to have remained in a ftate of perfect tranquillity. In 1070, William the Conqueror beftowed it, together with the Earldom of Hereford, on William Fitz-Ofborn. Odo, Bifhop of Bayeux, half brother to William the Conqueror, having determined, without confulting the king, to go to Rome for the purpofe of obtaining the Papacy, came to this Ifland in 1082, where he had caufed fome fhips to be prepared for his expedition. But the Bifhop being detained by contrary winds, and the king having been informed of his defign, came over from Normandy to the Ifle of Wight, and feized him with his own hands juft as he was going to fet fail. About two years afterwards the king went into the Ifle of Wight, and croffed from thence to Normandy. During his ftay in the Ifland, he levied very confiderable fums of money on the inhabitants, without paying much regard to the juftice of his claims.

In 1137, Baldwin de Redvers, Earl of Devonfhire, and Lord of the Ifle of Wight, having revolted againft king Stephen, was driven from his Caftle of Exeter, and purfued by the king into the ifland, from whence alfo he was in a fhort time compelled to fly.

The various events which occurred in England during the active reigns of Henry II. and Richard I. do not appear to have molefted the ifland.

In 1215, after king John had figned the great palladium of the liberties of England, *Magna Charta*, that monarch quickly formed a defign of annulling the grant ; and having fo recently experienced the extraordinary influence of the Pope over the minds of all men in that age of bigotry, he wifhed to engage the affiftance of the See of Rome in the execution of his project. Accordingly he fent a private letter to the Pope, wherein he intreated abfolution from the oath which he had taken to be faithful to his engagements; and left his defign fhould become public, and expofe him again to the refentment of the Barons and people of England before he was armed with ecclefiaftical fupport, he withdrew to the Ifle of Wight, where he waited three months for the Pope's anfwer, and the arrival of fome foreign troops which he expected. For fome time after his coming, he kept himfelf concealed from the obfervation of the inhabitants, amufing himfelf with the converfation of fifhermen and failors, with whom he became familiar in his walks upon the fea fhore, attended only by a few domeftics. After the Pope had annulled the great Charter and abfolved the king from his oath, John haftily quitted the ifland, and went to Dover to meet the foldiers, enlifted for him by his agents in Brabant, Flanders, and other places.

Henry III. granted the wardfhip of Ave-line, daughter and heirefs of Ifabella de Fortibus Countefs of Albemarle and De-vonfhire, and Lady of this ifland, to his fe-cond fon Edmund, who fhortly after married his ward.

King Edward I. was very defirous of purchafing the reverfion of the Lordfhip, and accordingly entered into a Treaty for that purpofe with his brother Edmund, and Aveline his wife, but before the purchafe could be completed, Aveline died without iffue in the life-time of her Mother. Edward, how-ever, found means to effect his purpofe, by perfuading the Countefs Ifabella to fell it for 6000 marks. The conveyance was made in the laft illnefs of the countefs; the deed was fealed about three o'Clock in the after-noon, and fhe died foon after midnight. This Deed, from the fufpicious circumftances attending its execution, was made an object of parliamentary examination in the fubfe-quent Reign of Edward II. upon the petition of Hugh de Courtney, Earl of Devonshire, who claimed the iſland as part of his inheritance from the counteſs Iſabella, to whom he was heir at law.

A ſhort time after this purchaſe, upon the breaking out of hoſtilities with France, the king iſſued a commiſſion appointing Sir Richard De Affeton, the Biſhop of Wincheſter, and Adam de Gorden, Wardens of the iſland, with orders for its defence, in caſe of an attack, which was expected to be made by the French upon the Southern coaſt of England.

Amongſt the many honours and eſtates beſtowed by Edward II. upon his favorite Peirs Gaveſton, when he married him to his neice Margaret, ſiſter to the Earl of Glouceſter, was Carisbrook in the Iſle of Wight, and with this was alſo conferred the wardenſhip of the iſland, of which, however, Gaveſton never obtained poſſeſſion.

In the 12th of Edward III. a writ was iffued to the Bifhop of Winchefter, ftating that the French, who had invaded the country about Portsmouth, and done confiderable mifchief, meditated fimilar depredations in the Ifle of Wight. The king, defirous on this account, that the ifland fhould be put in a proper ftate for defence, informs the Bifhop, that he has ordered the wardens of the ifland, to diftrain the lands and goods of all fuch perfons as failed to provide, agreeably to the tenure of their eftates, men at arms, and archers for the defence of the ifland. He alfo permitted the Prior and Monks of Appuldurcombe to remove to Hide Abbey, near Winchefter.

In confequence of thefe orders, fuch preparations were made for the reception of the enemy, that when they landed the following year at St. Helens, and were proceeding into the country, the Iflanders drove them back to their fhips, after an action, in

which Sir Theobald Ruffell, one of the Wardens, was killed. The regulations made at
this time for the fecurity of the inhabitants,
are quoted from a manufcipt in the poffeffion of Sir Simeon Stuart Bart. by Sir Richard Worfley, in his Hiftory of the Ifle of
Wight, from which very excellent work may
be collected many interefting particulars,
not compatible with the limited nature of a
publication, defigned only as an illuftration
of the views in the ifland.

The Governor, William Montacute, Earl
of Salifbury, and moft of the chief perfons of the ifland, received orders from Edward III. in the fifty firft year of his reign,
to provide for its defence; and writs were alfo
fent to the Juftices of the Affize, the Sheriff
of Hampfhire, and the Governor and Conftable of Carifbrook Caftle, directing them not
to compel the inhabitants to attend on
juries, in order that they might remain at
home for the defence of the place, which

(fay the writs), the public enemies wifh to get poffeffion of, and are preparing to invade*.

The expected invafion, however, did not take place, till the firft year of the fubfequent reign of Richard II. when the French, who had been repulfed at Winchefter, landed in the Ifle of Wight, and plundered all the inhabitants. On this occafion, the Caftle of Carifbrook was bravely defended by Sir Hugh Tyrril, who drew the enemy into an ambufcade, as they were approaching the Caftle, and killed a confiderable number. Finding themfelves at length difappointed in their hopes, the French withdrew from the ifland, after exacting a contribution of One Thoufand marks from the inhabitants, as a confideration for not deftroying their houfes.

* Quam etiam infula iidem hoftes multam defiderant, at cum infra breve tempus appropinquare et debellare proponunt ut audivimus et fe parant. RYMER, Vol. VII. p. 147.

In the fifth year of the reign of Henry IV.
the French again landed in the ifland, under the command of Valeran, Earl of St.
Pol, who having married the half-fifter of
Richard II. gave out that his attack was intended to revenge the death of that king.
However, the inhabitants, although they
received no afliftance from Henry, forced the
Earl to reimbark after he had plundered fome
of their villages.

Henry VI. about the year 1444, gave the
title of King of the Ifle of Wight to Henry
Duke of Warwick, and crowned him with
his own hand ; but it does not appear, that
the Duke obtained, with this diftinguifhed
honour, any regal power ; nor did he even
poffefs the Lordfhip of the ifland, which was
held, at that time, by Humphrey Duke of
Gloucefter, under a grant for his life.    It
has indeed been doubted, whether this unufual title was really conferred upon the Duke
of Warwick, as here related, but the fact may
be readily admitted, if we confider the high

degree of favour in which that nobleman ftood with King Henry, who was a weak prince, and in beftowing favours upon fo great a man, might have forgotten, or chofe not to regard, the impropriety of making a grant of the title of king, when, by the laws of the land, he was not enabled to transfer to another perfon the fovereignty of any part of his dominions. The fact, indeed, is confirmed, by a painting of the Duke, in an ancient window of the collegiate church at Warwick, where he is reprefented with a crown upon his head and a fceptre before him.

In the 28th of Henry VI. a petition from the inhabitants was prefented to the King, and another to the Parliament, complaining of the miferable and defencelefs ftate of the ifland which is attributed, by the petitioners, to the mifconduct of one John Newport, who had been fteward under the Governor, Richard Duke of York. It appears, that this Newport had been difcharged from his office, and had afterwards committed great depredations both by fea and land upon the property of the Inhabitants, though at the fame time he was making intereft at court to be reftored. The prayer of the petition was, that the ifland might be put in a ftate of defence, and that Newport might not be replaced in the office of Steward. But the King and the Duke of York were too much taken up with thofe fatal projects which fhortly after embroiled the houfes of York and Lancafter, to pay much attention to any reprefentations from a quarter fo remote from the fcene of action for which they were preparing. Happy indeed, in thofe days, were the Inhabitants of the Ifle of Wight, whofe fituation fecured them from participating in thofe wars of ambition which deluged England in blood!

During the difpute between Charles VIII. King of France, and the Duke of Bretagne, Sir Edward Woodville, uncle to Henry the Seventh's Queen, and Captain of the Ifle of Wight, defired the king's permiffion to raife a

troop of volunteers in the ifland, and carry
them to the affiftance of the Duke; but as
the king had himfelf offered to be mediator
between the contending parties, this propofal
was refufed. Woodville, however, notwithftanding this refufal, imagined the king would not
be difpleafed at his giving affiftance to the Duke.
He therefore repaired immediately to the ifland,
where he engaged about forty gentlemen,
and four hundred commoners, with whom
he fet fail from St. Helens, and joined the
Duke of Bretagne's army before the battle of
St. Aubin. In order to intimidate the enemy,
and make them believe that this reinforcement from England was greater than it
really was, the *Bretons* dreffed a large body
of their foldiers in white coats with red
croffes, which was the uniform worn by
Woodville's followers. The French however were not difmayed by this artifice, but
defeated the Duke's army in a dreadful battle,
in which Woodville and almoft all his
followers were flain. This battle was the
caufe of much affliction in the ifland, for

there was fcarcely a family of any defcription, who had not to lament the lofs of a relation or friend.

In the fourth of Henry VII. an act of parliament was paffed to prohibit the inhabitants from holding farms above the annual rent of ten marks. This regulation was adopted with a view to promote the population of the ifland, which had fuffered confiderably by Woodville's unfortunate expedition.

Henry VIII. in 1541, fent an order under his fign manual, to Richard Worfley Efq. captain of the ifland, to prevent the deftruction of game, and foon after the King went thither himfelf, and was entertained by that gentleman, at *Appuldurcombe*. Thomas Lord Cromwell, who was a principal inftrument in bringing about the reformation, was at that time conftable of Carifbrook Caftle, and attended the king in this excurfion, which was probably undertaken for the

purpofe of enjoying the diverfion of hawking,
which his majefty was extremely fond of.

In 1545, Francis I. king of France, fitted
out 150 large fhips, befides feventy fmaller
ones, and ordered them to fail towards
England. This fleet arrived on the 18th day of
July at the Ifle of Wight, under the command of Admiral Annebaut. The Englifh
fleet, which confifted only of fixty fhips,
lay at Portsmouth ; but they ftood towards
the enemy, and after a flight fkirmifh, retired
into the channel, in hopes that the French
would follow them and get entangled in
the fands and rocks. The French admiral
however was too prudent to attack them
in that dangerous fituation, and finding
the Englifh were not difpofed to give up
the advantage of their poft he landed his
forces in three different parts of the Ifle of
Wight, and burnt feveral villages. It was
even in contemplation of the French, to
fortify this ifland and keep poffeffion of it,
but finding that it would take more time

than they could fpare, and that the captain of the ifland (the fame Richard Worfley already mentioned) had taken meafures to drive them out, they departed very foon after their landing. For the future fecurity of the inhabitants, the captain caufed feveral forts to be erected on the ifland, and one of them was called Worfley's tower after his name. At fo early a period, this mode of fortifying might be confidered as a very fufficient fecurity againft the attacks of an enemy, but the modern improvements in the art of war (if any thing can be called improvement which tends to facilitate the deftruction of mankind) have been fo confiderable, that the ifland would now ftand but an indifferent chance, even from the attack of a large fhip of war, did it not find a ftronger protection than its forts, in that beft fecurity of Britain, its powerful and irrefiftible navy.

In the firft year of Queen Elizabeth, Richard Worfley, Efq. who had been difmiffed

from his office of captain in the preceding
reign, was reftored; and in his inftructions, he
was directed to take fpecial care for the increafe
of Harquebufry. In confequence of this
order, the ufe of fire-arms was firft introduced into the ifland.

In 1588, when England was in fome degree of alarm at the approach of what the
Spaniards called their invincible Armada,
this ifland, amongft the other feaports, was
put into as good a ftate of defence as time
would permit; but the meafures taken for
its fecurity by Sir George Carey, (the firft
Captain that affumed the name of Governor
of the ifland,) gave great offence to feveral of
the inhabitants, who remonftrated againft his
conduct to the Lords of the Queen's council.
But the danger of the times having rendered
ftrict regulations neceffary, their petition
was but coolly received, and Mr Robert Dyl-
lington, one of the petitioners, being charged
by Sir George with difaffection to the Government, was committed to the Fleet prifon.

Thefe gentlemen indeed were rather hafty in their condemnation of Sir George Carey, who, though he continued in the government many years afterwards, does not appear, in more peaceable times, to have perfifted in thofe arbitrary meafures of which they complained, and which might be juftified by the extreme hazard to which the ifland was expofed, at the period when he put them in practice.

It is at leaft true, that Sir John Oglander, in his MSS. memoirs written fome time afterwards, fpeaks handfomely of Sir George Carey's government, and draws a very ftriking contraft between the ftate of the ifland then, and in Sir George's time. The fingularity of fome of thefe remarks, may, perhaps, prove a fufficient excufe for introducing them in this place, in the author's own words.

" I have heard, "fays the writer," and partly know it to be true, that not only heretofore

there was no lawyer nor attorney in owre
ifland, but in Sir George Carey's time, an attorney coming to fettle in the ifland, was by
his command, with a pound of candles hang-
ing att his breech, lighted, with bells about
his legs, hunted owte of the ifland: infomuch
as oure anceftors lived here fo quietly and fe-
curely, being neither troubled to London nor
Winchefter, fo they feldom or never went
owte of the ifland; infomuch as when they
went to London (thinking it an Eaft India
voyage) they always made their wills, fuppo-
fing no trouble like to travaile."

Sir John afterwards obferves——"The Ifle of
Wight, fince my memory, is infinitely decayed; for either it is by reafon of fo many
attorneys that hath of late made this their
habitation, and fo by futes undone the country, (for I have known an attorney bring
down after a tearm three hundred writts, I
have alfo known twenty nifi prius of our
country tried at our affizes, when as in the
Queen's time we had not fix writts in a yeare,

nor one niſi prius in ſix years) or elſe
wanting the good bargains they were wont
to buy from men of war, who alſo vented
our commoditys at very high prices; and
readie money was eaſy to be had for all
things.  Now peace and law hath beggered
us all, ſo that within my memorie many of
the gentlemen and almoſt all the yeomanry
are undone."

Sir John's advice, which is ſubjoined, will
doubtleſs be thought better than his reaſon-
ing on the decline of the iſland. "Be adviſed
by me", ſays he, " have no ſuites at law ; if it
be poſſible, agree with thine adverſary, though
it be with thy loſſe : beſides the neglect of
thy time at home, thy abſence from thy wife
and children, ſo manie inconveniences hang-
eth upon a ſuite in lawe, that I adviſe thee,
although thou haſt the better of it, let it be
reconciled without law ; at laſt twelve men
or one muſt end it, let two honeſt ones do it
at firſte.  This country was undone with it,
in king James his reign ; hazard death and

all quarrels, rather than let thy tongue make his mafter a flave."

During the difpute between King Charles the Firft and the Parliament, before matters came to an open rupture, the Houfe of Commons, amongft other refolutions made in confequence of the news of a rebellion in Ireland, refolved, " that the cuftody of the Ifle of Wight be taken, for the prefent, from the Lord Wefton, fufpected of being a Catholic, and fequeftered into another hand." In confequence of this, Lord Wefton, who was alfo Earl of Portland, was removed from the government, notwithftanding the inhabitants prefented a petition to the houfe in his favour. The king, hereupon, gave the cuftody of the caftle of Carifbrook, to Colonel Brett; and the Countefs of Portland, together with her five children, and the Earl's brother and fifter, withdrew to the caftle, in hopes of being able to preferve it for the king.

The spirit of popular resentment, which had risen in most parts of England against that ill-fated monarch, spread itself also into this island; and the Newport militia, with four hundred men, collected from the ships in the port by authority of parliament, marched against the castle, under the command of Moses Read, mayor of Newport. Although the castle had a very slender supply of provisions, and there were not more than twenty men to assist Brett in its defence, the countess resolved to hold out to the last extremity, unless honourable terms could be obtained for the garrison. The castle, however, was soon after surrendered, upon condition that Colonel Brett, and those who had assisted in the defence should be allowed to go wherever they pleased within the island, and that the countess should be permitted to remain in her apartments at the castle, till the Parliament should direct the contrary.

It was not long, as might be expected, before she received notice to quit the island within two days, and after her removal, the parliament took poffeffion of the other forts, and the Earl of Pembroke, whom they had appointed governor, entered upon his office. This earl, is the fame who was returned, and took his feat in the Houfe of Commons, as knight of the Shire for the County of Berks, in 1649, after the fuppreffion of the Houfe of Lords.

In 1647, the king was feized by Cornet Joyce, and delivered up to the army, by whom he was foon afterwards fent to Hampton-Court. Finding the reftraint he was under at that place extremely difagreeable, as well as dangerous, he determined, with the affift-ance of his friends, Mr. Afhburnham and Sir John Berkley, to make his efcape, which he effected in the night, and, accompanied by them, and Legg, arrived fafe at Titch-field, in Hampfhire, a feat of the Earl of Southampton. At this place, they held a confultation, where the king fhould go next, and Afhburnham advifed, that he fhould re-

tire to the Ifle of Wight, and truft himfelf
in the hands of Colonel Hammond, who
was at that time governor, and whofe uncle
was one of his majefty's chaplains.   It fhould
have been confidered however, that Hammond had connections of a clofer nature
with the king's enemies.   He was married
to a daughter of the celebrated John Hamp-
den, and had been appointed governor of the
ifland, through the intereft of Oliver Cromwell.

Afhburnham and Berkley went firft to
the governor, to endeavour to make terms
with him ;  but all the anfwer they could
obtain, was, that he would do the king all
the fervice in his power ;  but as he was a
fubordinate officer, he could not undertake
to difobey his fuperiors in what they fhould
pleafe to command him. Hammond then went,
with Afhburnham and Berkley, to the king,
who returned with them to the Ifle of Wight,
and on the 12th of November, 1647, was
conducted to Carifbrook caftle, where Ham-

mond treated him with all poffible refpect, but fent a letter immediately to the fpeaker of the Houfe of Lords, acquainting him of the king's arrival in the ifland. His majefty alfo fent a meffage to the parliament, making propofals for an accommodation.

On the 14th of December, the parliament paffed four bills, to which they were defirous of obtaining the royal affent, before they proceeded in the treaty ; and for that purpofe they named a committee to prefent them to the king. The commiffioners from Scotland, who had attended the king at Hampton-Court, to treat relative to the affairs of that kingdom, protefted againft this proceeding of the parliament, and went to the Ifle of Wight to renew their negociations. They arrived there on the 25th of December, the day after the four bills had been prefented by the committee of the parliament. The Scotch commiffioners, having brought with them a treaty more agreeable to the incli- nations of the king, than the terms propofed by the parliament, he acquiefced in it, and told the committee, that he could not think of giving his fanction to any of the acts prefented to him, till the whole conditions of the peace fhould be concluded ; and for adjufting thefe, he knew of no way but a perfonal treaty, to take place either at London, or any other place the parliament fhould chufe.

Soon after the committee had received this anfwer, all the king's fervants were difmiffed from the caftle, and no perfon was permitted to fee him without an exprefs order. An attempt, however, was made by Captain Burley, an inhabitant of the ifland, to refcue Charles from his captivity ; but the plan was fo ill-concerted, that it was quickly difcovered, and ferved only to increafe the rigour of his confinement. Captain Burley himfelf was condemned and executed. But notwithftanding the fatal iffue of this project, two other attempts were made to effect this object, and the particulars are briefly as fol-

lows. Henry Firebrace, a perfon who, by permiffion of the parliament, came to attend the
king, as one of the pages of his bedchamber,
found means to deliver to him a packet of letters, written by fome who were favourable to
the royal caufe. This he effected, by placing
them in a fecret corner of the chamber, and
apprizing the king of the circumftance, by a
note conveyed into his majefty's hand as he
went to bed. The king took the difpatches,
and on the next day, put a letter in the fame
place, defiring Firebrace to continue that mode
of correfpondence, which indeed was fuccefs-
fully carried on for feveral weeks. A confiderable impediment, however, to the execution of any plan for the king's enlargement,
arofe from Colonel Hammond's having ordered two perfons to watch at the two doors
of the king's chamber during the day, whilft,
at night, their beds were placed fo clofe to
the doors that they could not be opened. But
Firebrace, having found means to ingratiate
himfelf with thefe guards, was allowed to
fupply the place of one of them, during fup-

per time, and thus found frequent opportunities of talking with the king. In one of thefe converfations, it was propofed, that the king fhould efcape out of the chamber window, after cutting the bars with a faw; but Charles, fearing that the noife of the faw would be heard, and conceiving that he might effect his efcape through the window of his apartment, without removing any of the bars, the diftance of which, from each other, was fufficient to afford a paffage for his head, determined on making the experiment, and accordingly directed that every thing fhould be prepared.

Mr. Edward Worfley, a gentleman of the ifland, Mr. Ofborne, another of the king's attendants, and Mr. Newland, of Newport, were made acquainted with the defign, and it was agreed, that, upon a fignal to be given from without, the king fhould let himfelf down by a cord, provided for that purpofe, and that Firebrace fhould conduct him to the main wall of the caftle, from whence he was to let himself down by another cord, into the ditch, out of which he could easily have ascended. Mr. Worsley, and Mr. Osborne, were to attend on horseback at this place, with a horse, boots, and pistols for the king, and Mr. Newland was to be ready at the sea-side, with a boat to convey him away.

Firebrace made the signal at the appointed time, and the king attempted to get out of the window, but unfortunately, when it was too late to provide a remedy, he found it impossible to get his body through the bars, and stuck so fast between them, that it was not without great difficulty that he extricated himself. Thus the king's design was frustrated; but his friends had, nevertheless, the good fortune to get away without its being known that such a plan had been in agitation. Firebrace, however, was afterwards dismissed from his attendance on the king, upon some circumstances of a suspicious nature, which had been communicated to Colonel Hammond.

Another fimilar attempt was afterwards made, but with no better fuccefs. The king had removed one of the bars, either by fawing it afunder, or by corroding it with aqua fortis, and was about to get through the window. But difcovering more perfons in the garden than he expected to fee, he thought it prudent to defift, and withdrawing himfelf, returned to bed. This plan had, in fact, been difcovered by Major Rolfe, an officer of the caftle, who had artfully deceived Ofborne into an opinion, that he would affift in liberating the king, and had, for that purpofe, been entrufted with a knowledge of the whole fcheme. It is faid, that Rolfe intended to have fhot the king as he came through the window, and that Colonel Hammond, had alfo placed foldiers to fire on the king's friends in their retreat, but they luckily efcaped unhurt. After this tranfaction, the king's confinement was rendered much more ftrict and uncomfortable, none of his friends or fervants being fuffered to approach him.

In September, 1648, after a long conten-
tion between the army and the parliament, it
was agreed, that a treaty fhould be entered
into with the king; and the town of Newport,
in the Ifle of Wight, was appointed for the
place of conference. The Houfe of Commons
fent inftructions to Colonel Hammond, that
the king fhould be removed to Newport, and
allowed the fame freedom he poffeffed at
Hampton Court; but no perfon who had
carried arms againft the parliament, was to
be permitted to fee the king, or to remain in
any fort or tower in the ifland. Accordingly his majefty was conducted to Newport,
and granted the indulgences directed by the
Houfe of Commons, upon giving his word
not to go out of the ifland during the treaty,
nor for twenty eight days after, without the
approbation of both Houfes of Parliament.

The commiffioners from both houfes, confifting of five lords and ten commoners,
being arrived at Newport, the conference
began on the 18th of September, at the

houfe of Sir William Hodges. But continual difficulties arifing in the courfe of the nego-ciation, the parliament feveral times found it neceffary to prolong the period allowed for the conclufion of the treaty; and the army, having, in the mean time, obtained a complete afcendency over the nation, deter-mined to put it out of the power of the parliament, to make any terms with the king, by feizing his perfon a fecond time. Fairfax, their general, in order to effect this object with greater certainty, directed Colonel Ham-mond to attend him at head quarters, and, at the fame time, fent Colonel Ewers to take the cuftody of the king.

On the evening of the 29th of November, the king was privately informed that the army intended to feize him, and fent for the Duke of Richmond, the Earl of Lindfay, and Colonel Cooke, to confult them, refpecting the mea-fures neceffary to be taken. After Colonel Cooke had communicated all the informati-on he had been able to get, by going to Carifbrook caftle, it was evident, the intelligence was well founded, and the king, was, on that account, advifed to make his efcape, which, under all circumftances, was thought a very practicable thing. But Charles rejected this advice, faying, " the parliament had promifed him, and he had promifed them, and he could not break firft."

At day-break, the king was informed, that there were feveral gentlemen of the army at the gate, who were defirous of fpeaking with him. Directions being given for their admiffion, the officers rufhed into the king's bedchamber, and informing him they had orders from the army for his removal to Hurft caftle, in Hampfhire, fcarcely gave him time to eat his breakfaft, before they hurried him thither ; nor would they allow the Duke of Richmond to accompany him farther, than about two miles on the road.*

* The occurrences of the night previous to King Charles's removal from the Ifle of Wight, are more fully related in Colonel Cooke's narrative, the original MSS. of which, is preferved in the Harleian collection, at the Britifh Mufeum.

After the reftoration, the inhabitants of the ifland prefented a petition to King Charles the Second, againft the governor, Lord Culpeper, whom they accufed of oppreffion, and of having neglected the fortifications of the ifland. But it was not fo well received as they expected, for Lord Clarendon, then lord chancellor, replied to their complaints by a letter, in which he blames them, both for the manner and matter of their petition.

In 1671, Charles the Second paid a vifit to the governor, Sir Robert Holmes, a very diftinguifhed naval commander, at his houfe at Yarmouth.

From this period, nothing occurs in the hiftory of the ifland, to which it is neceffary to draw the reader's attention. We fhall therefore proceed to give a lift of the lords, wardens, captains, and governors, in the order of time in which they were feverally appointed.

*Lords of the Ifle of Wight, from the time of William the Conqueror.*

William Fitz Ofborne,

Roger de Breteville, or Briftolis, Earl of Hereford. From the attainder of this earl, in 1078, the lordfhip continued in the crown, till Henry I. granted it to

Richard de Redvers, Earl of Devonfhire.

1135 Baldwin de Redvers, Earl of Devonfhire.

1155 Richard de Redvers, Earl of Devonfhire. (2)

1162 Baldwin de Redvers, Earl of Devonfhire. (2)

Richard de Redvers, Earl of Devonfhire. (3)

1184 William de Vernon, Earl of Devonfhire, and the Ifle of Wight.

1216 Joan, his daughter, who married Hubert de Burgh, Earl of Kent.

1227 Baldwin, Earl of Devonfhire. (3)
1240 Baldwin, Earl of Devonfhire. (4)

1257 Baldwin, Earl of Devonſhire, (5) and Amicia his wife, who held the lordſhip as part of her dower, after his death.

1283 Iſabella de Fortibus.

1293 The Crown.

1307 Peirs Gaveſton.

1308 Edward, Earl of Cheſter, afterwards Edward III.

The lordſhip afterwards remained in the crown till,

1386 William Montacute, Earl of Saliſbury.

1397 Edward, Earl of Rutland, afterwards Duke of York.

1415 Phillippa, Ducheſs of York.

1447 The Crown.

1449 Richard, Duke of York.

1452 Edmund, Duke of Somerſet.

1453 Henry, Duke of Somerſet.

1464 Anthony de Woodville, Lord Schales, afterwards Earl of Rivers.

1483 The Crown.

1485 Edward de Woodville.

It is uncertain whether this gentleman was lord or captain of the ifland ; but no grant of the lordfhip has been made fince his death.

1488 The Crown.

*Succeffion of Wardens, Captains, or Governors of the Ifland.*

The firft warden was appointed by the crown in 1216, during the minority of Baldwin, third Earl of Devonfhire. This appointment, indeed, has only exifted during minorities of the lords, or when the lordfhip happened to be in poffeffion of the crown, or of a prince of the blood royal.

1216 Walleran de Ties.

1229 Savery de Mauleon, or de Malo Leone.

1293 John Fitz Thomas.

1294 Richard de Affeton, the Bifhop of Winchefter, and Adam de Gorden. William Ruffell.

1302 Sir John Lifle.

1307 Nicholas Lifle.

Sir John Lifle again.

1321 Sir Henry Tyes.

1325 John de la Hufe, and John Lifle.

1325 Nicholas de la Felde.

1336 John de Langford.

1338 Theobald Ruffell.

1340 Abbot of Quarr.

1341 Sir Bartholomew Lifle, John de Langford, and Sir Theobald Ruffell.

1343 Bartholomew Lifle, John de Kingfton, and Henry Romyn.

1353 John de Gatefden.

1360 The Abbot of Quarr, Theobald de Gorges, and William Dale.

1377 Sir Hugh Tyrril.

1447 Henry Trenchard.

John Newport.

Henry Bruin.

1461 Sir Geoffery Gate.

1483 Sir William Berkley.

1483 Sir John Savile.

1485 Sir Edwarde Woodville.

1495 Sir Reginald Bray.

Sir Nicholas Wadham.

1511 Sir James Worſley.
1538 Richard Worſley, eſq.
1553 Mr. Giſling.
1558 Richard Worſley, eſq. again.
1565 Sir Edward Horſey.
1582 Sir George Carey, afterwards Lord Hunſdon.
1603 Henry, Earl of Southampton.
1625 John, Lord Conway.
1631 Richard, Lord Warton.
1634 Jerom, Earl of Portland.
1642 Philip, Earl of Pembroke.
1647 Colonel Robert Hammond.
1649 Colonel William Sydenham.
1660 Thomas, Lord Culpeper.
1667 Admiral Sir Robert Holmes.
1693 John, Lord Cutts.
1707 Charles, Marquis of Wincheſter, afterwards Duke of Bolton.
1710 General John Richmond Webb.
1715 William, Lord (afterwards Earl) Cadogan.
1726 Charles, Duke of Bolton.
1733 John, Duke of Montague.

1734 John, Vifcount Lymington, afterwards
      Earl of Portfmouth.
1742 Charles, Duke of Bolton, again.
1745 John, Earl of Portfmouth, again.
1763 Thomas, Lord Holmes.
1764 Hans Stanley, efq.
1766 Harry, Duke of Bolton.
1770 Right Honorable Hans Stanley, again.
1780 Right Honorable Sir Richard Worfley,
      Bart.

Having furnifhed a detail of as much of the hiftory of the ifland as is confiftent with the nature of this publication, it becomes neceffary, to revert to the village of Weft Cowes, of which fome defcription has already been given.

It remains only to be faid, that Weft Cowes is a Hamlet in the Parifh of Northwood. It has a chapel which was erected in the year 1657, probably about the period when Weft Cowes affumed the appearance of a village; as, before that time, it only confifted of a few fifhermen's houfes fcattered on the fhore. At this place, I embraced the opportunity of joining a party, who had engaged a veffel for the purpofe of making a voyage round the ifland.

The morning being fine, and the feafon the beft in the year for an aquatic excurfion, the furrounding country afforded that rich variety of tints which the approach of autumn ufually fcatters over the face of nature, and which contributes equally to delight the traveller, and inform the artift.

At fix in the morning we weighed anchor, and left Cowes Harbour, with a gentle breeze from the weft. We ftood out for the oppofite coaft of Hampfhire, where the lofty tower of Eaglehurft, backed by the luxuriant foliage of the new foreft, formed a ftriking and noble object. We now tacked and ftood in again for the Ifland, making the point of land on which ftands Mr. Collins's ,houfe, called Egypt, of which mention has already been made.

In Gurnet bay, we caught a picturefque inland view of the country, clofed with the high downs of Alvington, Bucombe, Mount-joy, and the caftle of Carifbrook. Here are feveral ftone quarries, which at prefent furnifh materials for the various improvements going forwards at Portsmouth. The rocks appear grand, and are well contrafted with underwood. On reaching Gurnet point we plainly faw, running to a confiderable length, the gravelly ridge, fuppofed to be the ifthmus which once joined the Ifle of Wight to Hampfhire.

We then put about for the Hampfhire fhore, and paffed the mouth of the river Bewley, from which we ftood acrofs to Thornefs Bay. The barrennefs of the fhore here, is much relieved by the farm at Whippence, and by woods ftretching towards this bay.

Another tack from the Hampſhire coaſt, brought us to New-town bay, into which runs the New-town river, by ſome called Shalfleet lake. The ſhore here lies very flat, without exhibiting any very ſtriking feature ; but Afton downs, which riſe behind the village of Shalfleet, form an agreeable back ground.

We found the ſhore from hence quite barren till we reached Yarmouth, which is ſituated on the water's edge. From the ſea, a battery, erected by Captain Urry at the bottom of his garden, ſtrikes the eye very agreeably ; and indeed might, at firſt ſight, be miſtaken for Yarmouth Caſtle, as it is by much the moſt conſpicuous. At the mouth of the river Yar, ſtands the caſtle, and the oppoſite ſhore is enlivened by the Hamlet of Norton, where the cottage of Mr. Binſtead, ſurrounded with fir and other trees, ſtands unrivalled. The view from it is extremely intereſting, as it commands Yarmouth roads, the uſual reſort of outward bound ſhips, together with the

Drawn & Engraved by Chas. J. Tomkins

Published as the Act directs Ja
nuary 1st 1795 by B and C Sandby Fleet Street

whole extent of the coaft of Hampfhire and the fhore of the Ifland, with Portfmouth and Spithead to clofe the fcene.

Paffing the fcite of Carey's Sconce, and Worfley's Tower, which are on Norton Common, we ftood over to Hurft Caftle. It is built on a neck of land, which runs out for a confiderable diftance, and forms that part of the Hampfhire Coaft which is neareft to the ifland, the channel being only three quarters of a mile acrofs. At this place the wind frefhened, and the agitation of our veffel convinced us, that we were croffing what the feamen call Fidler's Race. This unufual motion, which is always felt with a frefh breeze, is fuppofed to arife from the tide being confined in the narrow pafs.

On our approach to Cliff's-end, we made the land, and ftood clofe into Colwell Bay. The fhore here is bold, but fo barren as to afford little pleafure until we left Warden Ledge and Totland Bay; but, on ftanding round Headen Point, we entered Allum Bay, and were highly gratified with the fudden change, from a tame heath to ftately promontories of various colours, with which that part of the fhore abounds. At the extremity of the adjoining high lands, are feen the infulated rocks called the Needles. Three of them, of confiderable fize, are ftill remaining, but that which originally procured them their name, was a tapering pillar of above a hundred feet high, thrown down by the fury of the waves, in the year 1764. Its fall was attended with fo tremendous a fhock, that it is faid to have been felt at Southampton. The bafe of this rock we could not poffibly difcover, though the fea is particularly tranfparent at this part, and we employed a confiderable time in looking for it.

We ftood round the Needles, and lay to in Scratchel's Bay, which is the weftern end of the ifland. Here part of our company landed on the rocks, to take the diverfion of fhooting at their feathered inhabitants, which,

ALLUM BAY and the NEEDLES.

Drawn & Engraved by Chas. Tomkins.

Publication as Directs by Law & Sold by G. Kearsley, Fleet Street 1794.

in the months of May, June, and July, it is
said, are incredibly numerous. Whilſt my
fellow travellers were thus engaged, I rowed
out to catch a ſight of the Lighthouſe, which
is erected on the ſummit of the ſhore, for the
ſecurity of veſſels paſſing between the Needles
and ſome ſmaller rocks, lying more to the
northward, called the Shingles, and which
are ſuppoſed to have formerly joined. This
paſſage the ſailors call ſhooting the Needles.
When I had got out to a ſufficient diſtance
I made a ſketch of the *Weſt end of the Iſland.*

Scratchel's Bay is ſmall, and when viewed
from the beach, the rocks above have a ter-
rific appearance, as they overhang a conſiderable way, and their white colour adds
much to their apparent height. At the north
part of this bay, there is formed in the rock,
a natural arch, which at low water may
be paſſed on foot. Here we made a hearty
meal, and enlivened the dreary ſcene with mirth
and a bottle. We could not help obſerving,
that this is a ſpot by no means favourable to

the talents of our London fportfmen, who
were much deceived as to diftance on the
water. The birds, indeed, feemed aware of
this error, and remained quietly on the rocks
after being repeatedly fired at.

At length we embarked, and left this
bay with a fair wind, keeping the fhore, under Mainbench, which is a rock immenfely
high, faid to be upwards of fix hundred feet
perpendicular at high-water-mark. It is
chiefly compofed of light grey and white
ftone, in fome parts broken with yellow. In
the lower rocks we faw feveral fmall caverns,
but none of any confequence till we reached
Frefhwater-Gate. Our veffel again lay to,
and we took to the boat, intending to view the
cave of Frefhwater from its mouth; but this
we found impoffible, owing to the tide's
running in fo ftrong; and indeed, when a
wefterly wind prevails, it is highly neceffary to caution thofe travellers who do
not engage the man who refides at Frefhwater-Gate for a guide, to be very careful

how they approach the mouth of this Cave whilft the tide is running in ; for it requires a fkilful management of the boat to prevent mifchief, from the numerous rocks which are juft under the furface of the water. As we found the tide much too high to attempt entering it from the fhore, we returned to our veffel.

From Frefhwater Gate, we kept as clofe under the fhore as the rocks would permit, and paffed the parifhes of Brook, Mottefton, and Brixton. Their fhores do not poffefs any very ftriking features. On the contrary, a continued famenefs of dark loam, and yellow earths, tinged with green, in confequence of the quantity of copperas with which they are impregnated, rather offends than delights the eye. Copperas ftones, which are wafhed on this fhore every tide, and collected in great quantities by the inhabitants of the adjacent villages, are fhipped for London, for the purpofe of extracting the copperas.

( 126 )

We now ftood into the Channel, to avoid the lurking rocks which abound in Chale Bay. The dangers which thefe occafion to the unfufpecting mariner, though a fubject not the moft pleafing to contemplate, are neverthelefs fo beautifully and aptly delineated in the following lines, by an inimitable authorefs, that I cannot forbear introducing them here.

" Oft in this Bay—the dark o'erwhelming deep
   Mocks the poor pilot's fkill, and braves his fighs;
O'er the high deck the frothy billows fweep,
   And the fierce tempeft drowns the fea boy's cries."

" The madd'ning ocean fwells with furious roar :
   See the devoted bark, the fhatter'd maft,
The fplitting hulk, dafh'd on the rocky fhore,
   Rolls 'midft the howlings of the direful blaft."

" O'er the vex'd deep the vivid fulphur flies,
   The jarring elements their clamours blend,
The deaf'ning thunder roars along the fkies,
   And whiftling winds from lurid clouds defcend."

" The lab'ring wreck, contending with the wave,
   Mounts to the blaft, or plunges in the main ;
The trembling wretch, fufpended o'er his grave,
   Clings to the tatter'd fhrouds, the pouring rain

Chills his fad breaft, methinks I fee him weep,
  I hear his fearful groan, his mutter'd pray'r,
O, ceafe to mourn, behold the yawning deep
  Where foon thy weary foul fhall mock Defpair,
Yes, foon thy aching heart fhall reft in peace,
For in the arms of Death all human forrows ceafe."

Here our failors told us of an inhuman ftra-
tagem, faid to have been practifed on this
coaft for a number of years; but it has too
much the air of fiction and improbability
to be ferioufly credited. On every ftormy night,
the inhabitants of the coaft of Chale are faid
to have allured the unwary mariner to his
deftruction, by fixing a lanthorn to the head
of an old horfe, one of whofe fore legs had
been previoufly tied up. The limping gait
of the animal, gave the lanthorn a kind of
motion exactly fimilar to that of a fhip's
lanthorn, and led the deceived pilot on thefe
fatal rocks, a prey to mercilefs plunderers,
who, it is faid, would not even fcruple
to difpatch any unfortunate individual that
furvived the wreck, in order to fecure their
booty more compleatly.

On the high down of St. Catherine's, ftands
an ancient fea mark, which is perceived at a
confiderable diftance out at fea. The cliffs
under thefe downs, as you view them *en
paffant*, have the appearance of an immenfe
fortification; and on the fhore is a cavity,
which, though viewed at a diftance, ftrikes
the mind with horror at its dark and fable
afpect. This is called *Black gang Chine*, but
from whence it derived that name, our feamen
were unable to inform us.

We now ftood out to fea, to avoid the
fhoals of Rocken end, and in fo doing, part
of our company began to feel the unpleafant
fenfations of the deep water at the Race.
The fea, indeed, rolled tremendoufly, and
whilft our minds were impreffed with an idea
of its immenfity, we could have exclaimed
with an admired writer——

" Hail! thou inexhauftible fource of
wonder and contemplation! Hail! thou
multitudinous ocean! whofe waves chafe

Drawn & Engraved by Chas Tomkins.   Published as the Act Directs by C and G Kearsley Fleet St. 1795.

## BLACK-GANG CHINE.

one another down like the generations of
men, and, after a momentary fpace, are im-
merged for ever in oblivion ! Thy fluctuating
waters wafh the varied fhores of the world,
and while they disjoin nations, whom a nearer
connection would involve in eternal war, they
circulate their arts and their labours, and
give health and plenty to mankind."

" How glorious ! how awful are the fcenes
thou difplayeft ! Whether we view thee
when every wind is hufhed, when the morning fun filvers the level line of the horizon,
or when its evening track is marked with
flaming gold, and thy unrippled bofom
reflects the radiance of the over arching
Heavens ! Or whether we behold thee in thy
terrors ! when the black tempeft fweeps thy
fwelling billows, and the boiling furge mixes
with the clouds;—when death rides the
ftorm,—and humanity drops a fruitlefs tear
for the toiling mariner, whofe heart is finking
with difmay !"—

" And yet, mighty deep! 'tis thy *furface* alone we view.——Who can penetrate the fecrets of thy wide domain?——What eye can vifit thy immenfe rocks and caverns, that teem with life and vegetation?——or fearch out the myriads of objects, whofe beauties lie fcattered over thy dread abyfs?"

" The mind ftaggers with the immenfity of her own conceptions,——and when fhe contemplates the flux and reflux of thy tides, which from the beginning of the world were never known to err, how does fhe fhrink at the idea of that Divine Power, which originally laid thy foundations fo fure, and whofe omnipotent-voice hath fixed the limits where thy proud waves fhall be ftayed?"

Our attention was foon afterwards taken up, with viewing a convoy of upwards of two hundred fail of merchant fhips, working up the Britifh Channel; and the day being exceedingly fine, this fight was highly gratifying indeed. We now directed our veffel towards the ifland, and had a full view of the whole extent of what is termed the undercliff. This famoufly variegated and romantic part of the ifland is nearly five miles in length; and the information I received of its numerous and well contrafted beauties, was fuch, that I felt extremely anxious to land, in order to examine them. Wifhing however to complete our voyage on a day fo propitious to the undertaking, we fcudded under the fhore, which is compofed of clays of various hues, broke with numbers of fhrubs, and water falls interperfed with rock of feveral colours. The church of St Lawrence is feen from the fea, though a fmall and inconfiderable object. We next reached Steephill, where the Hon. Mr. Tolmarche occupies the houfe built by Hans Stanley, Efq. when governor of the ifland. The whole of this fcenery is backed by the cliff, which forms *Underwarth*, as it is called by the inhabitants, and the high downs of Niton, Week, Rue Ventnor, and St. Boniface. On paffing Ventnor, the Village of Bonchurch came full in view, the houfes of which are moftly whitewafhed; a common cuftom in the country, and which not only takes from the beautiful tints of nature, but difgufts the eye even when feen at a diftance. On this fubject, the opinion of that ingenious writer Mr. Gilpin, is fo perfectly conformable to my own fentiments, that I cannot help intro-ducing here, the remarks he has made con-cerning the impropriety of introducing white into landfcapes.

" Nature, fays he, never colours in this offenfive way. Her furfaces are never white. The chalky cliff is the only permanent object of the kind, which fhe allows to be her's; and this feems rather a force upon her, from the boifterous action of a furious element. But even here it is her conftant endeavour to correct the offenfive tint. She hangs her chalky cliff with famphire, and other marine plants; or fhe ftains it with various hues, fo as to remove, in part at leaft, the difgufting glare. The weftern end of the Ifle of Wight, called the Needle-cliffs, is a remarkable inftance of this. Thefe rocks are of a fubftance nearly refembling chalk;

but nature has fo reduced their unpleafant luftre by a variety of chaftifing tints, that in moft lights they have even a beautiful effect. She is continually at work alfo, in the fame manner, on the white cliffs of Dover; though her endeavours here are more counteracted by a greater expofure. But here, and in all other places, were it not for the intervention of foreign caufes, fhe would, in time, throw her green mantle over every naked and expofed part of her furface.

" In thefe remarks I mean only to infinuate, that *white* is a hue, which nature feems ftudious to expunge from all her works, except in the touch of a flower, an animal, a cloud, a wave, or fome other diminutive or tranfient object ; and that *her mode* of colouring fhould always be the model of *ours*."

" In animadverting, however, on *white objects*, I would only cenfure the mere *raw tint*. It may eafily be corrected, and turned into ftone-colours of various hues ; which though light, if not too light, may often have a good effect.

" Mr. Lock, who did me the favour to over-look thefe papers, made fome remarks on this part of my fubject, which are fo new, and fo excellent, that I cannot without impropriety, take the credit of them myfelf."

" White offers a more extended fcale of light, and fhadow, than any other colour, when near ; and is more fufceptible of the predominant tint of the air, when diftant. The tranfparency of its fhadows, (which in near objects partake fo little of darknefs, that they are rather fecond lights) difcover, without injuring the principal light, all the details of furfaces.

" I partake, however, of your general diflike to the colour; and though I have feen a very *fplendid effect* from an *accidental light* on a white object, yet I think it a hue,

which hurts, oftener than it improves the fcene.
It particularly difturbs the air in its office
of graduating diftances, fhews objects nearer
than they really are, and by preffing them
on the eye, often gives them an importance,
which, from their form and fituation, they
are not entitled to."

Leaving Bonchurch, we doubled Dunnofe, a craggy promontory, compofed of
dark earth, and rocks of a deep flate colour, tinged with green. It is fuppofed,
that a ftratum of coal runs from this point
to Bimbridge. In the rocks of Dunnofe,
there are feveral caverns, which the fmugglers,
a few years ago, made the depofitaries of
their contraband merchandize.

On paffing this headland, we fcudded clofe
under the fhore of Luecombe chine, and
reached Shanklin. Here the fcene from
the water is much enlivened, by the fhady
groves with which the village of Shanklin
abounds. Thefe, indeed, form a very agreeable

contraſt, which we did not fail to remark
for ſome hours before we reached them.
We lay to, oppoſite Shanklin chine, in order
to view this rural and extraordinary chaſm,
which is much reſorted to by thoſe who
make the tour of the Iſle of Wight. It was
a matter of regret to our whole party, that
time would not permit us to land. For my
own part, I ſhall not, in this place, attempt
to give the reader a deſcription of this char-
ming ſpot, as I ſhall have occaſion to mention it in the account of my progreſs through
the iſland, when I had a much better opportunity of contemplating its beauties.

As we paſſed on, the ſweep of Sandown
Bay, with Culver cliffs and Bimbridge point,
formed a new, and very pleaſing ſcene, improved by a very advantageous view of Mr.
Wilkes's cottage, in which that celebrated
gentleman has ſhewn the excellence of his
taſte in a variety of reſpects, and particularly
in ſelecting a ſpot, ſo peculiarly adapted by
nature as this is, for a ſummer reſidence.

For the protection of Sandown-Bay, Henry VIII. built a fort, which has been kept in good repair ever fince.

Sailing from hence, we came immediately under Culver-Cliff. In thefe rocks, which are compofed of chalk, a great number of gulls and common rock pigeons are bred; and the Cliff is fuppofed to have derived its name from this circumftance. About half-way up, is a place called Hermit's-Hole, which appears, at the diftance from which we faw it, to be a fmall cavity, only capable of being approached by a narrow and dangerous path, that defcends from the fummit of the rock, which, itfelf, is almoft perpendicular. Previous to, and during the reign of, Queen Elizabeth, there was, near this fpot, a famous breed of hawks, to protect which, the Governor had fpecial charge from the Queen, with directions to punifh any one who fhould prefume to plunder their nefts.

We now ſtood round Bimbridge-Ledge, and ſaw a richly cultivated country riſing above the Cliffs. A ſerene evening, and a declining ſun which gives an agreeable tinge to even the moſt indifferent objects, here added beauty to a ſituation at all times truly picturefque, and invited us to take advantage of the tide, and row up the Haven of Brading in a boat. Each ſide of this Haven is in a ſtate of high cultivation, and richly adorned with wood. The village of Brading, with its ancient church, forms a beautiful feature in the proſpect, which is backed by the high downs of Aſhey, on which is the ſea-mark directed by George II. A.D. 1735. This object is of great conſequence to the ſhips that paſs and repaſs from Portſmouth.

As we rowed back to our veſſel, we could not but admire the ſituation of the village of St. Helen's, which is on a riſing ground, on the north-ſide of the mouth of the Haven. On the ſhore, ſtand the remains of the old

church of St. Helen's, which has been dila-
pidated by various encroachments of the
fea. Part of the fteeple is faced with brick,
whitened, and ferves for a fea-mark for the
road of St. Helen's, which is juft off this
point, and is the ufual ftation of our fleets
when they leave Portfmouth or Spithead.

At a fhort diftance from this fea-mark,
commences a beautiful grove, belonging to
the Priory, a feat of Sir Nafh Grofe. Sailing in view of thefe woods, we entered Spithead, in order to have an opportunity of ob-
ferving the Britifh fleet, which lay at anchor
there. So grand a fight as this fleet, which
confifted of upwards of fifty large fhips,
with a numerous affemblage of fmaller veffels, could not fail to excite a degree of ex-
ultation, in the minds of Englifhmen, at the
aftonifhing naval ftrength of our country.
Nor, perhaps, were we to be thought inex-
cufable, in fo far giving way to a national
prejudice, as to imagine, that we difcovered a very vifible fuperiority in the conftruc-

tion and convenience, as well as the appearance and decorations of our ſhips of war, over thoſe of the Portugueſe Governor, which lay at Spithead at the ſame time.

We left this buſy ſcene, and ſtood over to the Mother-Bank, which is a ridge of gravel, lying about a mile to the north of the Iſle of Wight, and is the place where outward bound ſhips uſually aſſemble to wait for convoy, and where alſo the ſhips from the Straits perform quarantine. This ſtation is well adapted for the above purpoſes, as there is good anchorage, and various depths of water.

We now paſſed St. John's, a delightful villa, conſiſting of a ſmall but elegant manſion, built by the late General Amherſt. Immediately under it, is a ſeat of Mrs. Roberts, called Appley, which poſſeſſes the ſame advantages in point of ſituation, as St. John's. A little farther on, is Nettleſtone, the ſeat of Henry Oglander Eſq.; but of

this place, it is my intention to give a full
defcription in my tour through the ifland.

The next village on the fhore, is Ride, the
ufual place of embarkation from the ifland
to Portfmouth, where packets and open
boats are continually paffing. The wind
changing in our favour, we had an opportunity of directing our courfe under the
fhore of the Ifle of Wight, where we paffed
Binftead, and the woods of Quarr-Abbey,
to Fifhborn-Creek, which runs through
Wootton-Bridge, for fome diftance, into
the woods.

The fhore now continues wooded to
King's-Key, fo called, as I was informed,
from King John's having paffed fome months
at this retired fpot. On leaving this place,
the view is extended along the woods of
Barton-Point, to Old Caftle-Point, which
we paffed, and entered Cowes harbour,
much entertained with our voyage.

I landed again at Cowes, of which place
the reader has already been furnifhed with
a defcription, and commencing my journey
towards Newport, I afcended the hill,
from whence the road is enclofed with hedge
rows, which feparate it from well cultivated
lands on each fide, from Cowes to the
foreft of Parkhurft. About two miles
from Cowes, I turned out of the road,
to the left hand, in order to take the
view of *Northwood church*, which has a place
in this work.

The parifh of Northwood, is fituated on
the weft fide of the river Medina, oppofite to
Calfhot-Caftle. It is bounded by the fea on
the north and north-weft, by the parifh of
Calbourn on the weft, and by part of the parifh of Shalfleet, and the foreft of Parkhurft
on the fouth. The church of Northwood, was
a chapel of eafe to Carifbrook, until the reign
of Henry VIII. when parochial privileges
were granted to it, with an exemption from

GOODWOOD CHAPEL.

Published as the Act directs by G. and J. Robinson Pater Noster Row 1794.

contributing to the repairs of the mother church. But the great and fmall tythes ftill belong to the Vicar of Carifbrook, who is alfo Rector of Northwood. It is probable, that thefe tythes were of little value when they were originally affigned to the Priory of Carifbrook, as the parifh was at that time moftly over-grown with wood, and from this circumftance, it appears to have derived its name. The church, which is dedicated to St. John the Baptift, is built of ftone, and plaiftered in fome parts. It confifts of a body, compafs-roofed, and covered with tiles and ftone. On the north and fouth fides, there are ailes, which are feparated from the body, by four Gothic arches. None of the monuments in Northwood church are very ancient, or in any degree remarkable, except one, which has been erected to the memory of the Reverend Thomas Smith, who was minifter of this parifh, in the year 1681. It is formed of one entire piece of chalk, three feet long, and four feet high, curioufly carved with a variety of hieroglyphic characters, which are in high prefervation.

The chapel at Weft-Cowes, which has been already mentioned, is a chapel of eafe to Northwood, and is larger than the Parifh-church. It was confecrated in the year 1662, five years after its erection, by George, Bifhop of Winchefter; and was endowed, in the year 1671, with 5*l.* per annum for ever, by Mr. Richard Stephens. In the year 1679, Bifhop Morley endowed it with the further annual fum of 20*l.* upon condition, that the inhabitants fhould allow the minifter, (who is chofen by themfelves,) the fum of 40*l.* per annum; but if the inhabitants neglect to make this payment, the Bifhop's endowment is to be forfeited for ever. The rectory of Northwood, is united with the vicarage of Carifbrook, and both are in the gift of Queen's-College, Oxford. The annual amount of the poor's rate collected in this parifh, is about 360*l.*

Before the Reformation, there was, in this parifh, a religious houfe of " fratres et forores fraternitatis fancti Johannis Baptiftæ, in ecclefia de Northwode," brothers and fifters of the fraternity of St. John the Baptift, in the church of Northwood. This monaftery was fituated near the church, but it had not fubfifted long, before it was fuppreffed, with the other eftablifhments of that fort, by Henry VIII. The building, which is faid to have been ftanding about a century ago, was called the *Church-houfe*, but no remains of it can be traced at prefent.

Near Northwood Church, is the neat and hofpitable cottage of Captain Price, which commands an interefting view of the river Medina ; and not far diftant, is Medham, the feat of Mr. Green, which poffeffes the fame advantages in point of fituation.

Returning from Northwood, I purfued the Newport road for a mile and a half, till I came to the gate of Parkhurft foreft. The view before me was extenfive ; commanding, towards the left, the river Medina, with its cultivated fhore; in the front appeared St. George's down, backed by St. Catherine's down ; and, on the right, Carifbrook Caftle, with Mountjoy, and the high downs fur-rounding it.

The foreft of Carifbrook, or Parkhurft, is extra-parochial, and contains about three thoufand acres of land. In the reign of William the Conqueror, and for a long time afterwards, it was called the King's Park, and is fo defcribed in domefday book. By a grant made in the twentieth of Henry VI. to Henry Trenchard, of the office of conftable of Ca-rifbrook, it is denominated the King's Fo-reft ; and in an account of rents, iffues, and dif-burfements of the ifland, in the twenty-third of Henry VII. there is a charge for falaries paid to the ranger of the foreft, and two un-der keepers. Swain-motes were yearly held in this foreft, as appears by a warrant from the duke of Suffolk, juftice of the king's forefts, parks, and chaces, in the thirty-fixth of Henry VIII. directed to the warden, lieutenant, and quarter keepers of the foreft of Carifbrook.

About a mile within the foreft, ftands the houfe of induftry for this ifland, a ftructure, which, for convenience and good regulation, is equally deferving of praife and imitation. The poor who receive the advantages of this ufeful inftitution, are much indebted to the humanity and good fenfe of the gentlemen of the ifland, who, at a general meeting in the year 1770, propofed an application to parliament, for confolidating the poor rates of the feveral parifhes, and erecting a houfe or houfes of induftry, for the maintenance and employment of the indigent. In confequence of the unanimous opinion of this meeting, and the meafures afterwards purfued, an act of parliament was obtained in the eleventh year of his prefent Majefty's reign, the preamble of which fets forth the ufeful purpofes it was intended to effect. It ftates " that the providing a place for the general recep-

tion of the poor, would tend to the more effectual relief of such as by age, infirmities, or
diseases, were rendered incapable of support-
ing themselves by their labour; to the better
employment of the able and industrious; to the
correction and punishment of the profligate
and idle; and to the education of the children
in religion and industry; and thereby making
the poor, instead of being totally supported
by the public, contribute to the support, af-
sistance, and relief of each other; and be of
some advantage to the community, to which
they had before been only a heavy and griev-
ous burthen." By this act of parliament,
His Majesty was enabled to grant, under the
exchequer seal, such part of the forest of Parkhurst, near the town of Newport, not exceed-
ing eighty acres, as certain trustees therein
named, should allot for the purposes of the
act, for such term as his Majesty should think
proper. The trustees having fixed upon a
spot which they thought the most convenient
for the intended building, obtained a grant
of eighty acres to be made to the corporation

erected by the act, for the term of nine hundred and ninety-nine years, at the yearly rent of £.8 17 9¼. Agreeably to this plan the houſe of induſtry is erected ; the principal part of the building extending from eaſt to weſt three hundred feet, and twenty feet wide, with windows on both ſides, for the benefit of a thorough air. A wing twenty-four feet wide is formed from the main building, at the diſtance of two hundred feet from the weſt end, and extends in length, towards the ſouth, one hundred and ſeventy feet. A range of workſhops alſo, for manufacturers and mechanics, runs from the end of this wing in a line parallel with the main building. On the eaſt ſide of the wing is a court, one hundred and ſeventy feet by fifty, having a dairy, waſhhouſe, brewhouſe, and other offices on the eaſt ſide, and a wall on the ſouth.

The principal building conſiſts of a ſtore room, ſteward's room, committee room, a dining hall one hundred and eighteen feet

long, and twenty-feven feet wide, a common
fitting room for the aged and impotent poor,
rooms for the laundry, governor, and matron,
nurferies and fick wards, with excellent cellars under the eaft end. On the ground
floor of the wing, are the governor's and matron's fitting rooms, the fchool rooms, apo-
thecary's fhop, kitchen, fcullery, &c. Above,
are the lying-in rooms, fick wards, twenty feparate apartments for married men and their
wives, and two common fitting rooms for
the old and infirm. In front of the principal building is a large gateway, on the eaft
fide of which is a mafter weaver's room and
fpinning room, with ftore rooms over them ;
and on the weft fide, are the fhoemaker's and
taylor's fhops, and a large fpinning room,
with weaving rooms, and ftore rooms in the
upper ftory. The manufactures now carried on are, facks for corn, flour, and bifcuit;
ftockings kerfeys, and other articles of ap-
parel for the ufe of the poor. On the north
fide of the principal building is a chapel, fifty feet long by twenty feven wide, where di-

vine fervice is performed twice a week, befides
Sundays. There is alfo a peft houfe, and a
burial ground walled in. A large garden,
which fupplies the houfe with vegetables, occupies the ground on the fouth fide of the
building ; and on the eaft, behind the offices,
is a barn, a ftable, hog-fties, &c. The houfe
is capable of containing near feven hundred
perfons, and the number ufually fupported in
it, are from five hundred to five hundred and
fifty, varying according to the feafon, and the
general healthinefs of the country.

The great expence of this building, which
exceeded the fum allowed by the act of parliament, made it neceffary, in 1776, to pro-
cure a fecond act, by which the corporation
was enabled to borrow a farther fum of money. Many defects in the former law were
alfo remedied, and the corporation of guardians were continued, with new and enlarged
powers. By this act the corporation are fty-
led, " The guardians of the poor within the
Ifle of Wight," and all perfons are declared

to be guardians, who poſſeſs, in their own right or in right of their wives, lands within the iſland rated to the poor rate at the yearly value of 50*l*. or are heirs apparent of ſuch lands of the yearly value of 100*l*. or rectors and vicars within the iſland, or who are occupiers of lands rated at the yearly value of 100*l*. Out of theſe, twenty-four directors and thirty-ſix acting guardians are annually appointed for the management of the concerns of the corporation, and in them is veſted the appointment of proper officers for the internal government of the houſe. That part of the land which is not occupied by the building and garden, has been cultivated at a very conſiderable expence, and is divided into fields of from five to twelve acres, moſtly fenced with quick hedges, and in ſuch a ſtate of improvement as promiſes to repay very amply, the labour and coſt beſtowed on them.

I have been induced to give a more circumſtantial account of this excellent inſtitu-

tion than is perhaps confiftent with an undertaking like the prefent, merely from a
conviction, of the great benefits which the
public would derive, from fimilar eftablifhments in different parts of the kingdom.

Not far from the houfe of induftry, is St.
Crofs, the feat of Mr. Kirkpatrick. Upon
this fpot formerly ftood a priory or hofpital, dedicated to the Holy Crofs. It is mentioned in the Lincoln Taxation 20th Edward I. and again, amongft the alien priories,
in the twenty-fifth of the fame reign. This
priory was a cell to the abbey of Tirone, in
France ; but by whom it was founded is not
known. It appears to have been called an
hofpital in the 6th of Richard II. that monarch having granted " to John de Cowef-
hall, the cuftody of the *hofpital* of the Holy
Crofs, in the Ifle of Wight, for life."

An acknowledgement was paid to the priory of Carifbrook, from this houfe, for the liberty of burying their own dead, for which the

bifhop had granted a licence. This being an alien priory, was given to the college of Win-chefter, fome time before the general diffolution of the religious houfes. Some fmall remains of the ancient building, are ftill vifible in the walls of Mr. Kirkpatrick's houfe, and the farm-houfe adjoining.

From St. Crofs, I took the view of the "*Entrance into Newport*", which appears in this work.

The town of Newport is confidered as the capital, and ftands nearly in the centre of the ifland. It is watered on the eaft and weft fides by two ftreams, one of which takes its rife at the foot of St. Catherine's, and the other at a place called Rayner's grove, about three miles from Newport: thefe two ftreams, after fupplying feveral corn mills, form a junction at the quay, from whence the river Medina is navigable to the fea. The town contains about fix hundred dwelling-houfes, and is difpofed in five long

Drawn & Engraved by Chas. Smith.

Published as the Act Directs by C. Smith, Kinsley Hall 1794.

parallel ſtreets, croſſed by three others, the
whole of which are well paved. The buildings, which are for the moſt part of brick,
are neat and regular, and amongſt them are ſeveral good houſes. To the beauty and amuſement of the place two elegant aſſembly rooms
alſo contribute. In the original plan of the
town, it was intended, that there ſhould have
been three large ſquares, at the interſections of
the ſtreets, to ſerve as markets for cattle, corn,
and poultry ; but various encroachments have
deſtroyed the uniformity of the firſt deſign.

A market is held every Wedneſday, and
another on Saturday. The principal com-
modities brought thither, are poultry, but-
ter, and grain. A great part of the latter, is
manufactured in the iſland, into flour, malt,
and biſcuit, for the navy ; and the remainder
is ſold for exportation.

Newport received its firſt charter of immunities from Richard de Redvers, the ſecond

earl of Devon of that name, in the reign of Henry the fecond. The fecond charter was granted by Ifabella de Fortibus, countefs of Albemarle and Devon.

In this charter, the countefs ftyles the town her new *borough of Medina*; and fhe grants to the burgeffes, all the market tolls, and other liberties belonging to her; with power of diftraining for fuch tolls, and of holding pleas, and amercing within the borough. She alfo grants the burgeffes common of paf- ture for all animals in Parkhurft; and fhe gives them in fee, a water mill, near the pri- ory of the Holy Crofs, called Weft-mill; and a moiety of another water-mill, fituated near the Ford, called the Ford-mill.

A yearly rent of eighteen marks, is referved to the countefs, and one mark annually to the lepers of the hofpital of St. Auguftine, for all the houfes in the borough, except certain meffuages, with their appurtenances, which are ftated to have been dedicated, by the

countefs, to God, and the chapel of St. Nicholas in the caftle of Carifbrook, and to the
vicar of that chapel.

Thefe premifes are ftill out of the jurifdiction of the borough, and are called " Caftle-
" hold." The rent referved for the mills,
tolls, fines, and amerciaments, is eighteen
marks of filver to the countefs, and two
marks annually, to the prior and monks of
Carifbrook.

The borough of Newport fent reprefentatives to the parliament held in the 23d
year of the reign of Edward I ; and it appears,
that writs were fent to the bailiffs of the Ifle
of Wight, in the fecond and fourth years of
the reign of Edward II ; but no returns were
made to the fheriffs upon thofe writs.

The charter of Ifabella de Fortibus, was
fucceffively confirmed, by Edward III. Richard II. Edward IV. Henry VII. Henry VIII.
and queen Elizabeth ; by fome of whom

were added, grants of the forfeitures of out-
laws, felons, and fugitives, within the borough, and of the petty cuſtoms within all
ports and creeks of the iſland.

By ſome of the old books of the corporation, it appears, that they formerly claimed
fourpence per ton, from all ſhipping which
paſſed the coaſt ; and this is ſuppoſed to have
been the origin, of the duty ſtill impoſed on
all veſſels anchoring in Cowes road, at the
mouth of Newport river.

King James I. granted a charter to the
bailiff and burgeſſes of this borough, conſti-
tuting them a corporation, to conſiſt of a
mayor, twenty-four burgeſſes, and a recorder : the mayor to be ſworn in before the
captain of the iſland, or his ſteward. The
mayor, recorder, (or his deputy) and two burgeſſes, are impowered to hold a court every
Friday, for the trial of all cauſes of debt, treſ-
paſs, &c. ariſing within the borough.

In the thirteenth year of Charles II. the mayor and burgeſſes obtained a ſecond charter, by which they are now incorporated by the names of the mayor, aldermen and burgeſſes. The aldermen, who are twelve in number, are elected by the mayor and aldermen, out of the chief burgeſſes; and the mayor is elected out of the aldermen. The petty cuſtoms within all ports and creeks of the iſland, are confirmed to the borough by this charter; and the mayor, aldermen, and burgeſſes, are exempted from ſerving on juries.

No members were ſent to parliament by this borough, from the twenty-third of Edward I. until the twenty-ſeventh of Elizabeth; but, from that period, they have been regularly returned. Newport is indebted to Sir George Carey, captain of the iſland, for the reſtitution of this privilege; and the gratitude of the bailiff and burgeſſes, appears from a memorandum entered in the town books, by which they acknowledge the favour done them by Sir George, and agree, that he shall nominate one of the burgesses during his life.

The steward of the governor of the island, holds a court in the town hall, called " Curia " militum, knight's court, or knighten " court." This court is of very ancient institution, and is supposed to have been erected by William Fitz-Osborne, who received the first grant of the island from William the Conqueror. It is plain, that this court is of feudal origin; for the judges of it were such as held a knight's fee, or part of a knight's, from the lord of the island; and these judges, according to the feudal system, gave judgment, as in courts of equity, without the intervention of a jury. The captain's steward or his deputy, holds this court, by virtue of the captain's patent, every Monday three weeks, except that day happens to be a holiday. It has jurisdiction over the whole island, except the borough of Newport, and holds plea of all actions of debt and trespass under the value of forty shillings, and upon replevins

granted by the steward or his deputy. The
proceedings are of the same nature as those
in our courts of equity, and are carried on by
attornies admitted by the court. The actions
of debt are tried by proof of plaintiff or defendant, or the defendant's wager of law, by
two hands, if he prays it, and actions of tref-
pafs are determined by proof only.

A reprefentation was made to lord Conway, the governor, in 1626, concerning the
nature of this court, and the inconvenience
arifing from the fmall number of its judges,
who muft be freeholders, holding of the caftle of Carifbrook. This was alfo accompanied with fome ufeful hints for its improvement, by the introduction of juries, and the
extenfion of its jurifdiction to caufes of
higher value. No alteration, however, has
been made in its forms or powers.

The feal of Knighton Court reprefents
a caftle with battlements, round which are
infcribed thefe words :

SIGIL: CVRIÆ MIL: IN: INSVLA: VECTIS:+:

Under the government of the earl of Southampton, in the beginning of the laſt century,
a free grammar ſchool, was erected at Newport,
by public ſubſcription. It is a plain ſtone
building, with convenient apartments for the
maſter, who is maintained by the profits
ariſing from ſome lands adjoining to the
foreſt, which were granted in fee to the
bailiffs and burgeſſes of Newport, in the firſt
year of Henry V. by Agnes Attelode, and
John Erleſman, at the yearly rent of twenty-
pence. The original deed of conveyance is
kept in a ſmall black box in the town-cheſt,
and is as follows :

"*SCIANT preſentes et futuri qd. nos* Agnes *qui
fui uxor* Johannis Attelode *et* Johes. Erleſman
*ſenior dedimus conceſſimus et hac pnti. charta nra.
confirmav.* Willmo. Farſye & Willmꝉ. Gandere *ballivis de novo burgo de Newporte* Johanni
Compton, Johanni Langſtoke, Willmo. Paxhulle, Richard Shide, *et oibus. alijs burgens,
ejusdem burgi omnes terras et paſturas quas ha-
mus. Sup.* Honiehulle *in borial pte. curſus aque
voc.* Lukkeley *et in occiden. pte. foſſat. priorat.*

*See* Cruc. *voc.* Monken Woodich : *habend. et tenend. omnes terras et paſtur. prtas. cum ptin. ſuis prefatis* Willmo. Farſye, Willmo. Gandere, Johanni Compton, Johanni Langſtoke, Willmo. Paxhulle, Rico. Shide, *et oibus. alijs burgens. burgi præd et heredibus ſuis imppm. ꝺe capital. dnis feodi illar. p. ſervic. inde debit. et de jure conſuet. Reddend inde annuatim nobis et heredibus nris. viginf. denar. ad feſt. Paſche et ſee* Michis. *arch. p. equales porcones. pro oibus. al. ſervic. exaĉtionibus ſive demand. Et nos vero predic.* Agnes *et* Johes Erleman, *et heredes nre. oes. prdtas. terr. et paſtur. cum ſuis ptin. prefatis* Willmo. Farſye, Willmo. Gandere, Johanni Compton, Johanni Langſtoke, Willmo Paxhulle, Rico. Shide, *et oibus alijs burgenſibus predic. burgi et heredibus ſuis contra oes. gentes warrentiꝗ .ꝗim. acquietabim. et imppm. defendem. In cujus rei teſtimon. huic preſenti charte nre. ſigilla nra. appoſuim. Hijs teſtibus* Willmo Bremeſkete, Willmo Ringborne, Thome Brereding, Johanne Hakett, Johanne Heyno, *et alijs. Dat. apud* Newporte *pred. qrto. die menſis Octobris anno regni regis* Henrici Quinti *Primo.*".

The church ſtands in the centre of one of the ſquares. It is ſuppoſed to have been built about the reign of Henry II. from its being dedicated to St. Thomas à Becket, who was the popular ſaint of that time. The building is of ſtone, and is ſpacious, but not ſufficiently lofty for its ſize. It conſiſts of a body and two ailes, one of which is ſeparated from the body by ſeven gothic arches, and the other by ſix. It has been imagined that this church was partly built by a ſubſcription of the mechanics who reſided in the town, from the various mechanical figures carved on the South wall, ſome of which are ſtill viſible; but it is probable many more have been deſtroyed by the ſucceſſive reparations of the church. The tower has a ring of ſix bells, and is provided with a clock. The pulpit is of wainſcot, ornamented with fourteen emblematical figures curiouſly carved in alto relievo, repreſenting the Liberal Arts and Cardinal Virtues. Under the founding board is the date of 1636, and on the cornice, a ſentence from Iſaiah, cut in fret work. On the top, the God

of War and the Goddefs of Peace are reprefented, forming an union. The church
has galleries all round, and likewife an
organ. The only monument in it worthy of
notice, is that of Sir Edward Horfey, who is
reprefented in armour, lying in a handfome
decorated niche. At his feet is a horfe's head
attired in a wreath argent and azure, and
above him is the following infcription :

*Edwardus qui miles erat, fortiffimus Horfey,*
*Vectis erat præfes conftans, terraque marique*
*Magnanimus, placidæ fub pacis nomine fortis,*
*Juftitiæ cultor quam fidus amicus amico.*
*Fautor Evangelii, dilectus principe vixit*
*Munificus, populo multum dilectus ab omni*
*Vixit; et ut fancti, fic ftamina fancta peregit.*

*Qui obiit 23 die Marcii.*
*An. Dni 1582.*

The arms of Sir Edward are quartered
over the centre of the arch.

Sir Edward Horfey well deferved the praife
beftowed on him in this Epitaph. During
feventeen years government of the ifland, he

was conftantly attentive to its interefts, and particularly to the wool trade, from which it derives confiderable advantage. There is extant, an agreement between the bailiffs of the town of Newport, and the clothiers of the county of Somerfet, for fixing the petit cuftoms of wool, purchafed by the clothiers within this ifland; this agreement is dated the 6th of July, 1578; and is declared to have been made by the mediation and award of Sir Edward Horfey. The plentiful fupply of game with which this ifland formerly abounded, was alfo owing to the attention and care of this gentleman, who is reported to have been fo anxious for its increafe, that he gave a lamb to every perfon who brought a live hare into the ifland.

The chancel is feparated from the body of the church by fmall oak pillars and arches ornamented with carving. In digging a grave nearly under the communion table for the honourable Mr. Weft, fon of Lord Delawar, in October 1793, the leaden coffin of

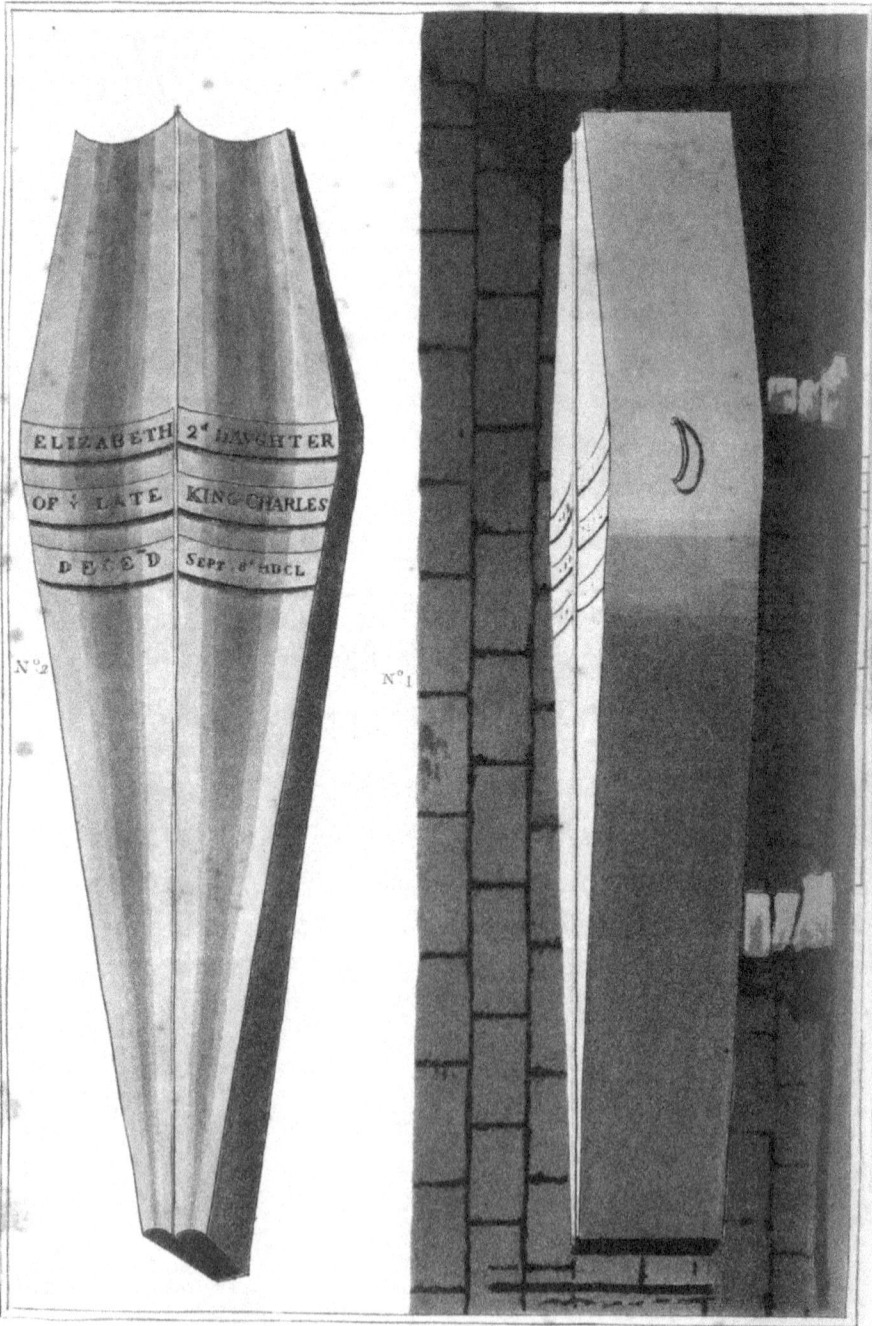

N.º 2

ELIZABETH  2.ª DAVGHTER

OF ý LATE  KING CHARLES

DECE'D  Sept. 8.º MDCL

N.º 1

Princefs Elizabeth, fecond daughter of King Charles I. was difcovered in a vault which was perfectly dry when it was opened, and the coffin in a ftate almoft equal to new. An ingenious friend having communicated a fketch of the coffin, taken in the fituation in which it ftood when the vault was opened, the reader will probably not be difpleafed with the annexed engraving of it. Fig. 1, in this Plate, fhews the coffin in a fide view, as it ftood in the vault; and Fig. 2, the lid with the infcription. Upon the wall of the chancel not far diftant from the vault, is a fmall ftone, with the letters E. S. cut in it. This obfcure infcription had paffed almoft without notice, till the coffin was difcovered, but it now feems clear, that it was meant as a direction to thofe who might fearch for the grave of this unfortunate young Princefs, Elizabeth Stuart, who did not long furvive her father, and died a prifoner in Carifbrook Caftle.

Newport originally belonged to the Priory of Carifbrook, and upon the fequeftration

of the Priory, the right of appointing the
minifter feems to have devolved, as in all
fimilar cafes, to the vicar of the Mother
Church of Carifbrook: and this appears the
more probable, as there is no endowment of
the Church of Newport, nor, indeed, was
there any certain fupport for the minifter till
the year 1653, when the mayor and chief
burgeffes ordained, that a rate fhould be
made for his fubfiftence. As the minifter is
thus entirely fupported by the inhabitants,
it has been ufually left to them to elect
whom they pleafed; but judging from the
ufual courfe of ecclefiaftical preferments,
we are rather naturally led to agree with Sir
Richard Worfley, that the appointment of
the curate is ftrictly in the vicar of Carifbrook. From the report made to Edward VI.
by the commiffioners appointed by letters
patent in 1547, it appears, that the plate,
bells, veftments, and other implements belonging to the Church of Newport, which
were feized at the Reformation, produced the
fum of £100. 5s. 6d.

The great increafe of buildings in Newport, fince the decay of Carifbrook, has extended the town beyond the limits of the
parifh. Accordingly, Caftle Hold is within
the parifh of St. Nicholas, Copping's Bridge
is in that of Whippingham, and Node Hill
in Carifbrook.

Newport has given title to four Earls and
one Baron. In the fourth year of Charles I.
Lord Mountjoy Blount, natural fon of the
Earl of Devonfhire, was created Baron
Thurlfton, and Earl of Newport. He was
fucceeded by his three fons, who all dying
without iffue, the title became extinct
in 1679.

The borough of Newport fends two burgeffes to parliament. The right of election
is in the corporation, confifting of twelve
aldermen and twelve burgeffes ; who have
been for fome time paft influenced in their
choice of reprefentatives, by the family of
Holmes. Upon the death of the late Lord

Holmes, his eftate in the ifland, together
with his influence in this borough, defcended to his Nephew the Rev. Leonard Troughear, who has taken the furname of Holmes.
An attempt was made, at the time of Lord
Holmes's death, to change the patronage of
the borough; and a confiderable intereft was
eftablifhed in the corporation, by Sir William Oglander and fome other gentlemen,
for the purpofe of effecting this object.
There were at that time only twenty-three
electors, eleven of whom had declared themfelves in favour of the old patronage, and an
equal number were determined to oppofe it.
The remaining elector was Mr. Taylor of
Newport. Both parties in their zeal to fecure this gentleman's intereft, applied to him
in a way that gave him an opportunity of exhibiting a character, for integrity and in-
dependence, rarely to be met with in the
annals of borough elections. He was offered
a confiderable fum of money by the agents
of each party; but difdaining to put to fale
that which is juftly confidered the moft va-

luable privilege of an Englishman, he chose
rather to refign his gown as a burgefs, than
give his fupport to any party who would ac-
cept his fuffrage on fuch difhonourable terms.
Since this event, Mr. Troughear Holmes,
found means to eftablifh himfelf in the patronage, and ftill continues to poffefs it.
The prefent members are, Lord Vifcount
Palmerfton, and the Hon. Penyfton Lamb.

The town of Newport is badly fupplied
with water, there being few wells. On this
account, the principal part of the water ufed
by the inhabitants, is brought in water-carts
from Carifbrook, and retailed through the
town. It appears however, that, formerly,
there was a better regulation in this refpect;
for in digging lately in the beaft-market for
ftone to pave the town with, a large refer-
voir was difcovered, and feveral pipes have
likewife been found in the road from Carifbrook, leading in a direct line to Newport.
It would be very eafy to reftore this method
of fupplying the town with fo neceffary an
article; and it is fomewhat furprizing, that

this fhould have efcaped the notice of thofe
public fpirited gentlemen, who have, on
many occafions, taken great pains for the
improvement of the ifland, and the accommodation of its inhabitants. It is faid, indeed, that a gentleman offered a fhort time
fince to bring water by pipes from Carifbrook, and alfo to light the town, if the corporation would elect him one of their reprefentatives in parliament : and though elections of this fort ought to be free from influence of every defcription, it muft be allowed that this was fuch a propofal, as might
have been accepted, without fubjecting the
electors to the fame degree of venality, as
would have attached to the acceptance of
fuch an offer as that rejected by Mr. Taylor.
The advantages in one cafe would have been
materially felt by the public; in the other,
the avarice of an individual alone would have
been gratified.

There was formerly at Newport a chauntry, dedicated to the Bleffed Virgin, and
founded by John Garfton of that town. By

a half yearly rental, beginning at Michael-
mas in the year 1682, it appears, that the
lands in and about Newport, belonging to
this chauntry, were in the poffeffion of Edward Fleming Efq. the yearly income thereof,
at that time, being £15. 3s. 6d. The fame
lands are now held by John Fleming, Efq.
who pays to the crown the yearly rent of
£12. 5s. 9d.

The original feals of the town, made ufe
of under the charter of Ifabella de Fortibus, and the firft feal ufed by the corporation,
under the charter of King James I. are ftill
remaining. The former of thefe reprefents
an ancient fhip, with one maft, and a fail
bent, and an anchor and rudder. Round it
is this infcription:

**Sigillum: commune: uille: de:
Neuport: in: Infula: de:
Wight.**

King James's feal is made of copper, and is in two pieces, formed fo as to be fcrewed into one handle. One part of it is kept by the mayor, and the other by the town clerk; confequently the feal cannot be made ufe of without the prefence or affent of the poffef-fors of both parts. It reprefents the figure of the King in full face, in his royal robes, with a crown on his head. On one fide of the figure is the letter I, on the other the letter R; and furrounding the feal, is this infcription:

S'STATVTORVM MERCATOR' CAPT' INFRA BVR-GVM DE NEWPORT IN INSVLA VECT.

I fhall clofe this account of Newport, with a copy of the charter, granted to this town, by Ifabella de Fortibus, in the reign of King Edward the Firft.

" *Sciant prefentes et futuri, quod ego* Ifabella de Fortibus, *comitiffa Albemarl. et Devon. ac Dna. Infulæ in ligea viduitate et plena poteftate*

mea, dedi et conceſſi, et hac preſenti charta mea
confirmavi burgenſibus meis de novo burgo meo de
Medina omnimodam libertatem de theolonio, et de
omnibus alijs conſuetudinibus unde liberi burgenſes
libertatem habeant, quantum in me pertinet ; per
totam terram meam, in villis, in vijs, in terra, in
mare, in portu, in nundinis, in mercatis, in ven-
ditionibus, in eruptionibus, in burgo et extra burgum, et in omnibus locis, et omnibus rebus ſuis.
Conceſſi etiam præfatis burgenſibus meis qd. ſint
quieti et liberi de ſciris et hundredis, et de omnibus ſect. ad ſeir. et hundr. in inſula. Conceſſi
quoq. ijſdem burgenſibus qd. habeant comia paſ-
turæ ad omnimodo animalia ſua p. totam paſturam
in landis meis in Parkhorſt, extra boſcum quie-
tam de herbagio in perpetuum. Præterea conceſſi
ipſis burgenſibus, quod omne placitum quod in pre-
dicto burgo ortum fuit, quod ad me pertinet in ipſo
burgo inter ipſos et per ipſos placitetur et amer-
ciamentum inde proveniens, per ipſos amercietur et
taxetur. Et volo et concedo pro me et hæredibus
meis qd. nullus eorum cum amerciari debeat
de amerciamento qd. ad me pertinet, ad
plus quam ad triginta denarios amercietur;

*et hoc judicis et confideratione ipforum bur-
genfium conceffi infuper prædictis burgenfibus
qd. nullus in dicto burgo fit præpofitus aut balivus
nifi ipfe quem ijdem burgenfes et hæredes eorum
reddent fingulis annis mihi et hæredibus et affig-
natis meis pro omnibus meffuagijs fuis in eadem
villa exceptis meffuagijs ædificatis in tredecim placeis et dimid. placea quorum redditum una cum
efcheata et omnibus alijs rebus adhuc unde contin-
gentibus dedi et conceffi Deo et capellæ beati Nichi.
in caftro meo de Carefbroc et vicario ejufdem capellæ prout carta ejus plenius porteftatur, ad duos anni
terminos decem et octo marcas duos folidos et duos
denarios, viz. medietatem ad Pafcham, et alteram
medietatem ad feftum fancti Michis: et leprofis
hofpitalis fancti Auguftini ad prædictos terminos
fingulis annis unam marcam argenti de libera et
perpetua eleemofina mea, videlicet ad quemlibet
terminorum prædictorum dimid. marc. Dedi infuper et conceffi prædictis burgenfibus meis ad feodi
firmam perpetue duratur unum molendinum aqua-
ticum fitum juxta prioratum fcti. Crucis qd. ap-
pellatur la Weft Mill, cum omnibus ptinentijs fuis,
et medietatem unicus molendini aquatici fiti juxta.*

*ta ford quod vocatur Le Ford Mill, cum omnibus ptinentijs suis. Concessi etiam qd. præfati burgenses quiete habeant omnia et fingula amerciamenta de omnibus querelis et placitis ortis in prædicto burgo quæ inter ipsos placitantur vel placitari possint. Et etiam qd. habeant totum theolonium et custumam quæ ad me pertinent in prædicto burgo et extra burgum, simul cum potestate distringere pro eisdem theolonis et custuma, in omnibus locis ubi ea aliquando tempore consueverunt, exceptis tredecim placeis et di mid. supradictis et salvis libertatibus a me concessis abbati et conventui de Quarr. et hominibus suis, priori Xti ecclesiæ de Twynham, et hominibus suis, et priori de Appledurcombe, et hominibus suis, prout cartæ eorum plenius et melius testantur ; habendum et tenendum omnia premissa data et concessa prædictis burgensibus et eorum hæredibus, cum omni commoditate et incremento quæ in prædicto burgo accessere poterint ; sine contradictione reclamatione seu impedimento mei, vel hæredum aut assignatorum meorum, libere, pacifice, quiete, et integre, reddendo inde annuatim mihi et hæredibus vel assignatis meis pro prædicta feudi firma molendin.*

*theolon. cuftum. et amerciament. decem et octo marcas argenti ad quatuor anni tempora, viz. ad feftum fcti. Michs. fexaginta folidos, ad nat. Dni. fexaginta folidos, ad feftum Pafcb. 60s. et ad nat. fcti* Johis. Baptiftæ, 60s. *Et priori et monacis de Carefbroc, duas marcas annuatim ad eofdem terminos per æquales portiones de perpetua elee- mofina pro omnibus fervitus fæcularibus exactione et demandis. Et ego* Ifabella, *et hæredes et affig- nati mei hæc omnia data conceffa et confirmata prædictis burgenfibus et eorum hæredibus in om- nibus et per omnia warrantizabimus et contra omnes gentes defendemus in perpetuum : ut autem hæc noftra donatio et hujus cartæ meæ confirma- tis perpetuæ firmatis robur obtineat, præfentem cartam figilli mei impreffione roberavi. Hijs tef- tibus,* Willō. de Sancto Martino, Henrico Trenchard, Thoma de la Haulde, Tho. de Evercey, Willō. Eftur, Jordō. de Kingefton, *militibus,* Johē. de Patghgrave, *tunc conftabu- lario infulæ,* Johē. de Heyno, Willē. de Nevile, Galfrido de Infula, Hugone la Vavafur, Walt. Barnard, *et aliis."*

The prefent number of inhabitants of the town of Newport, is two thoufand feven hundred and feventy-eight.

The extenfive tours to which we now proceed to draw the reader's attention, fhall be defcribed in the following order, viz. Firft, the Weftern; Secondly, the Eaftern; and Thirdly, the Southern; each of which poffeffes a great and pleafing variety. Before we commence with thefe, however, it may not be amifs to point out two walks, in the vicinity of the town of Newport, that will give the traveller a juft idea of the fituation and conveniences of the place: thefe will alfo prove a confiderable faving to him in point of time, and render it lefs necef-fary to digrefs from the general road of the different tours that we fhall have occafion to mention in future.

The Medina being the fource of the mer-cantile advantages of Newport and its en-virons, it feems requifite to direct the reader's notice to a walk on the banks of that river; an excursion which cannot but be pleasing to all visitors of the Isle of Wight. The way to the river is down Quay-street; then across a foot-bridge, near Mr. Cook's Brew-house, over the stream that runs from Carisbrook, and joins the Medina river at this place. After passing a few fishermen's houses, we are then led by a path between a double row of elms, on the bank of the river. The most eligible time for undertaking this walk, is the evening, when the beauties of this delightful scene are viewed to the greatest advantage. At the end of the path, we enter a copse, which still possesses a pleasant gloom, and at various openings shews the river and its opposite banks, which are covered with a fine verdure. Leaving the copse, we take the beaten path up an easy ascent in the adjoining meadow, to a seat placed under a clump of trees, from whence we have an extensive view in every direction. The southern view wears so picturesque an appearance, that I have

Drawn & Engraved by Chas. Tomkins.

Published as the Act Directs by Cundee & Tomkins Soho London 1796.

MEDINA RIVER.

been induced to give a reprefentation of it, under the title of *The Medina River*.

This place is much reforted to by the inhabitants of Newport. A fhort diftance from it, is a pleafant fpot, called Hurft-ftake, which is a fmall Public-houfe, under a grove of trees, on a projecting fweep of the river's banks. Refrefhments may be procured here, and likewife a boat for crofsing the river, which fhould rather be done at this place than farther on ; as this fide of the river now begins to lofe its agreeable variety. From this fituation, the ferpentine direction of the river is feen to advantage in either view, and is no lefs worth attending to than the rival mills, fituated on each fide of the river. Thefe are immenfe piles of brick and ftone work ; and though far from picturefque, do not deferve on that account, to be paffed over in filence, fince their want of beauty is amply compenfated by their utility. They are faid to be capable of grinding forty loads of wheat in a week; and

are worked by a pent water, which is formed
by the tide's flowing over a dam. Thefe
fabrics alfo poffefs every convenience for
baking bifcuits for the ufe of the navy, of
which confiderable quantities are daily fhipped for Portfmouth, and other places.

The principal kinds of fifh which are
caught in the river Medina, are mullet,
flat-fifh, and oyfters.

Croffing the water at Hurft-ftake, the tide
running out afforded fo advantageous a view
of the place I had juft left, as to induce me
to add a fecond plate under the fame title.
In this view *Hurft-ftake* forms the right-hand
fcreen, and the Whippingham fhore the left,
with Newport Church, and the high ground
of *Mountjoy* in the centre.

At Fairlee, in the parifh of Whippingham, is the feat of John White, Efq. On
the eaft-fide of the river, the houfe is fub-
ftantial, and has the appearance of being a

Drawn & Engraved by J.C. Stadler

Published in the Sketches by Samuel & Stanley Harbour 1795.

Drawn & Engraved by John Smith.

Published as the Act directs by Vernor & Hood, Poultry, Feb.ʸ 1799.

good family houfe. It is built of glazed brick, plain, and without decoration, as may be perceived from the annexed view of the weft front, which is taken from the lawn, that falls, in an eafy flope, towards the water's edge. At the fouth-fide of the lawn, is a plantation of evergreens, under a grove of oaks, in which is a winding path from the water up to the houfe.

Leaving this place, we took the right-hand path into the fields, in one of which the view of *Newport from Fairlee* was drawn. This is a much better view of the town of Newport than is feen in any other direction; as it exhibits the whole of the town, backed by Mountjoy, Carifbrook caftle and village; befides Bucombe, Avington, and Galibury Downs, with the grove of St. Crofs: in a word, the river only is wanting to make this view complete. Paffing the meadows, we entered the Whippingham road, and kept to the right-hand which led by Coppin's-bridge into the town of Newport, and were not a little satisfied with our excursion.

Carisbrook Castle deserves likewise to be recommended for a walk, as it is not more than a mile from the town of Newport. The way to this place is through High-street and Castle-Hold, taking the foot-path called the Mall, which joins the western end of the town. It is about two hundred yards in length, and eight yards wide. On the left hand, it is in part shaded by lofty elms, under which, some seats would be a very desirable addition. On the right, it is open to meadows, which are backed by Parkhurst forest. It possesses also the farther advantage of a good view of Mountjoy, Carisbrook Castle, the village of Carisbrook, and Priory Farm: from its contiguity to the town, it is the resort of the gay throng.

At the end of this walk, is the horse-road to the village of Carisbrook, and to the

Published by J. Hinton Newgate Street ... 1764

caftle. Juft oppofite to this part of the road, is a narrow lane, which is the pafs where, it is faid, Sir Hugh Tyrrel, in 1377, defeated the French, who were on their march to the caftle of Carifbrook. The lane ftill retains the name it acquired from that event, of *Deadman*'s lane; and adjoining the Eaft end of it is a part of Newport, called Nodes hill, probably a corruption from *Noddies* hill, which was the name given to the tumulus, formed by the bodies of thofe flain in the engagement. Farther on, the road divides at an angle: the left leads to the caftle, and the right to the village, both of them carriage roads. At a fhort diftance, for the accommodation of foot paffengers, there is an agreeable path over the fields, which continues by an eafy afcent, till you arrive at the outer gate of the caftle. This road is much improved, and the wafte ground, which is planted with various fhrubs, will, in a few years, form an agreeable contraft with the furrounding fields and meadows.

These meadows produce a plant, which is not commonly met with, called the *Ophrys apifera*, or *Bee Orchis*. The stalk and leaves of this plant resemble those of a hyacinth; and, at the top of the stalk, it bears a double flower, so extremely like a bee, that the naturalists have observed, that all other insects, deceived by the appearance, forbear to approach it.

**END OF THE FIRST VOLUME.**

CPSIA information can be obtained
at www.ICGtesting.com
Printed in the USA
BVHW041806220819
556561BV00022B/5295/P

9 781314 996555